The Art of Selling Memberships

How I've Sold Millions of Dollars in Gym Memberships and How You Can Too

By Erik Charles Russell

For online training visit this website:

www.membershipsalesacademy.com

You should follow me on social media here:

Twitter: twitter.com/erikcrussell

Facebook: facebook.com/erikcharlesrussell

Instagram: instagram.com/erikcharlesrussell

FREE BOOK UPDATES AND VIDEO TRAINING

This book is INTERACTIVE – to get free training videos, access to more resources, updates, and upgrades to this book when new versions or editions are released:

Text me

aosmupdates

to

(678) 506-7543

The Art of Selling Memberships

ISBN-13: 978-0-578-15931-7

Dedication

Kevin Seaman, my adopted father. He helped me develop confidence and channel my fighter mentality towards positive outcomes. He gave me my first job selling memberships.

To my beautiful wife, Tyne McCreadie. She's the best sale I ever made. And believe me, it took pie charts, bar graphs, and the whole nine to get her and to keep her by my side. She is proof that I can sell!

To my daughters, Kiera and Kylie. They keep my sales skills sharp every day by forcing me to extol the features and benefits of why listening to me is important.

To all of the members of my gyms and everyone I have ever sold a membership to. Thank you for your time and trust. I couldn't have written this book without the experiences that you shared with me.

Finally, I dedicate this book to all of the salespeople who have listened to and implemented what I have taught them. You are the proof that *The Art of Selling Memberships* will work for anyone who applies it.

Table of Contents

Introduction

It was my first week on the job. A woman came into the gym where I was working and told me she was going to die. The woman was on the verge of tears. She was obese, she had diabetes, and she was depressed.

Earlier that day she had visited her doctor. Her doctor told her that she needed to start taking her health more seriously or she would die before her time. He recommended that she eat better and start exercising.

In basketball, the best way to guarantee two points is to jump up and to slam-dunk the ball through the hoop. It's virtually impossible to miss a slam-dunk! In sales, every once in awhile you get your opportunity for a slam-dunk sale, the sale that is virtually guaranteed. This was going to be "that sale" and the easiest commission that I ever made.

She had the recommendation from her doctor. She had significant motivation, death. And here she is in the one place that can solve her problem and help her live a long, healthy life ... my gym!

We talked for a bit and I gave her a gym tour. As part of our gym tour, we always gave the prospect a free initial training session that was meant to get their heart rate up a bit and familiarize them with the club. The trainer that I paired her up with that day was very good. He knew just how to guide her through her first workout.

Despite not having any prior training experience she did great during her first session. She even looked like she was having fun, which was a far cry from the depressed state that she came to me in. This wasn't going to be a just any slam-dunk sale. This was going to be some LeBron James slam-dunking type of sale!

As the workout ended, I go up to her and ask, "So, what do you think?"

"Oh, I loved it," she replies.

"That's great," I said. "Let's go to the office and get your membership squared away."

"Sure!"

She followed me to the office and I proceeded to show her the membership options that were available. I showed her the standard membership, the super standard, the gold standard, and the diamond elite membership. Of course my recommendation was the diamond elite, that's the one that I made the most money selling. Then I did what my manager taught me and what his manager taught him, I assumed the sale.

"Now, what membership option will you be signing up for today and how would you like to pay for it?"

"You know, I appreciate everything that you did for me today. I'm definitely going to be joining your gym. Tomorrow."

"Tomorrow?"

"Yes, that's a lot of options and I've got to look at my budget. Plus I have to talk to my boyfriend. So let me think about it and I'll get back to you."

I was stuck. I thought to myself, "What does she need to think about? Her doctor told her she was going to die! She knows she needs to do this."

This woman had just told me that she loved the workout. She told me how much fun it was. She told me that her doctor said that she needed to do it for her long-term survival on this planet. She walked out the door.

I called her on that "tomorrow day." I didn't get an answer or a return phone call. I called again and again and got the same result. No answer, no return phone call, and no sale. It was the easiest sale that I never got.

I had someone who was literally dying to get my services and I couldn't close the deal. My future in this business didn't look very bright. Based on my pay scale of 100% commission, I was going to have a career earnings total of zero dollars. Something needed to change and it did.

I became obsessed with learning how to sell. I studied from the greats. Tom Hopkins, Brian Tracy, Zig Ziglar, Roger Dawson, Anthony Robbins, Jeffrey Gitomer and more. I studied psychology, neuro-linguistic programming, and body language. I read books, listened to audio cassette tapes, and went to seminars.

It's been 20 years since I lost that first sale. In that time, I've sold millions and millions of dollars worth of memberships to people from all walks of life. I've taught others my process and have seen them achieve similar results.

What I'm about to share with you, I have never shared with the public. It's the process that I have developed through all of those years of studying, practicing, and more importantly applying what I've learned.

It's a sales process and philosophy that is built around the prospect. You uncover their needs, wants, and motivations. Then you show them a solution to their problem through a membership at your studio, gym, or fitness center. Not only will you close more membership sales with this process but also your prospects and members will love you for it.

ARE YOU READY TO BECOME OBSESSED?

Learn The Art of Selling Memberships directly from me at the Membership Sales Academy. Membership Sales Academy is the most comprehensive, in depth, and easiest way to improve your selling skills.

Grow your understanding and your income by joining me at membershipsalesacademy.com.

I'll see you there!

Selling Memberships Is An Art

The year was 2009. I owned multiple locations of martial arts schools and fitness centers. My sales staff consisted of eight full-time salespeople. Each year I would take my staff to some kind of field trip for a little business training and little rest and relaxation. Those trips were a lot of fun and I always tried to find something interesting and different to do. That year, I decided to take my team to a small town called Merion, PA just outside of Philadelphia.

Merion, PA was home to The Barnes Foundation, now located at the Philadelphia Museum of Art. The Barnes Foundation was an educational institution based on private art collection of Dr. Albert C. Barnes. Dr. Barnes developed a drug in the 1900's that made him a millionaire and in 1910 he dedicated himself to the study and collecting of art.

After more than a decade of buying and collecting art from all over the world, in 1922 Dr. Barnes had a mansion built in Merion to display his collection.

The collection consists of 69 Cézannes — more than in all of the museums in Paris — it also has 60 Matisses, 44 Picassos, and 178 Renoirs. The 2,500 items in the collection also included major works by Henri Rousseau, Modigliani, Soutine, Georges Seurat, Edgar Degas, and Vincent van Gogh, among others. The estimated value of this collection is $20 to $30 billion. Yes, billion. The foundation's assets are more valuable than the assets of the Carnegie Corporation and the Rockefeller Corporation combined and multiplied by five.

After receiving harsh criticism for his taste in art by the established art critics, Dr. Barnes created numerous restrictions to limit the number of visitors he would allow to view this art collection. Almost 90 years later, those restrictions were still in place. Through numerous emails and phone calls, I managed to get a tour with my sales team.

As we arrived on the steps of the mansion, I explained to my team what they were about to experience. The building that we were about to enter had the most valuable collection of anything that they had ever witnessed in their lives and probably ever will witness for the rest of their lives. They were about to experience pieces of art that had never been revealed to the world at large. Dr. Barnes wouldn't allow anyone to photograph the paintings. If you didn't see them in person, you didn't get to see them at all.

Not one member of my team knew anything about art. They didn't even care about art other than the fact that I told them they were about to see billions and billions of dollars worth of it up close and personal.

I explained that I just wanted them to walk through and appreciate what they could appreciate. I knew if they just walked through with an open mind, some piece from one of these master artists would speak to them.

We walked through the different rooms of the mansion and we saw the Van Goghs, the Picassos, the Renoirs, the Matisses, and more. Each piece of art was hanging on those walls without barriers or behind some type of protective glass. It actually made me a bit nervous thinking of the possibility of someone from my sales team tripping and falling through one of this multi-million dollar pieces of art!

Thankfully, nobody tripped and fell into any artwork. After the tour, I gathered my staff together in my hotel room. One by one I asked them if any of the art caught their attention. They not only had one piece that impacted them but they had multiple pieces that they were inspired by.

Then I asked them how they thought that these artists were able to create art that even people who had no previous interest, now remembered and were inspired by.

The truth is that anybody can go get a canvas, some paint, and a brush, just as these masters did. Anybody can take a brush and physically put that paint on the canvas just as these masters did.

What separates the masters from everyone else? What makes one person's art memorable, inspiring, and ultimately worth millions while another is worth less than what they paid for the canvas? Before you read my answer below, think about it for a minute. What is your answer?

Every painter has a canvas. Every painter has a brush. Every painter has multiple colors to choose from for their painting. The difference between the masters and the amateurs is not the paint that they put on the canvas but the passion that they put on the canvas.

Their heart, their soul, their pain, their pleasure is on that canvas. Their everything is there for you to see and experience. They put everything they have into their work. It's so deep and profound that it is almost impossible to not be moved and inspired by it, even with very little understanding of art. This is why people all over the world will pay millions of dollars to own a single piece.

I say to you as I said to my team that day. You have your canvas, your paint, and you have your brushes. They are in your hands and in front of you right now. It's your gym, your programs, your abilities, your talent, and your heart.

Selling memberships is an art. The heart, the soul, and the passion that you put into the art of selling memberships will determine whether you create a masterpiece worth millions or whether you're just another salesperson.

Master this art and you will be able to write any amount that you wish on your paycheck. You will never have to worry about how to pay your bills or where your money comes from. It will come from your art, the art of selling memberships.

FREE BOOK UPDATES AND VIDEO TRAINING

This book is INTERACTIVE - to get free training videos, access to more resources, updates, and upgrades to this book when new versions or editions are released:

Text me

aosmupdates

to

(678) 506-7543

Your Gym Is Your Gem

You've finally found the "one." She's everything you could ask for. She's smart, she's beautiful, and it just feels like she completes you as a person. It's time to ask her that scary question, "will you marry me?"

Not so fast though. Before you pop the question you need that significant piece of jewelry that seals the deal like no other, the engagement ring. You know this. That's why you've been saving your money so let's take a trip to the jewelry store and do your woman right.

There's a bunch of jewelry stores in your area but this location in particular is close and convenient so you decide to stop in. You pull into the parking lot and notice that the outside façade of the store is nice and the store signage is attractive. You're excited and a bit nervous.

When you walk in, nobody is there to greet you. You start inspecting the surroundings. On the floor you see lint and little pieces of paper. You see dirty footprints here and there. You notice that the jewelry display cases are all dusty, dirty, and disorganized. The glass has streaks, it has spots, and even worse, the glass has fingerprints all over them.

Then the janitor appears from the back of the store. At least he looks like the janitor. His hair is a mess and his clothes are shabby. You'd like to offer him some hygiene and style advice.

The guy introduces himself as Vinny. He says that he'll sell you whatever you like cheaper than any other store around. Vinny tells you to look around and to yell to him when you find something that you like. Then off Vinny goes to the back of the store again.

As soon as Vinny is out of sight, you leave the store quicker than when you walked in.

Picture in your mind for a moment of how successful you think that particular jewelry store would be if those were the standard conditions every time somebody walked in. Or even of those were the conditions every once in awhile. I'm sure you see them struggling to be successful.

And Vinny? Vinny goes on to complain about how "window shoppers", people who look but don't buy, take up all his time. If only good customers would walk into his store. Customers who could appreciate good jewelry for the lowest prices in town, he'd be able to make some money.

Off to another store you go. The next store you arrive at isn't as convenient but it looks just as nice on the outside as any other. You walk in and it's like a completely different world.

You are greeted at the door by a friendly salesperson named Giovanni. Giovanni thanks you for coming to his store and expresses his excitement in meeting you. You tell him that you want to look at engagement rings.

You notice that he is dressed very well, almost too well. His suit looks freshly pressed. The hair on his head is groomed to perfection. He's wearing one of the nicest watches you've ever seen and his pinky ring puts most engagement rings to shame.

Giovanni gives you a personal tour of the store. The fresh carpeting on the floors doesn't have a speck of lint or dirt on them. You see clean, well-lit displays. The glass that houses the jewelry is in fact so clean and spotless that it looks like there is no glass there at all. Everything is sparkling from everywhere. You thought buying an engagement ring was going to be expensive, now you know it is.

Picture in your mind how successful you think Giovanni and his jewelry store are. Compare the experience that you had there to the first experience that you had. You almost don't even want to think about the first guy.

According to statisticsbrain.com the average gym membership dues paid in the U.S. are $58 per month. That's almost $700 per year. In some cities like New York, NY, Savannah, GA, and Naples, FL average membership costs are over $130 per month or more than $1,500 per year.

If you do your homework, you'll find that the average jewelry buyer spends $726 per piece. That's according to industryIQ.biz. That is in the same price range for what they are paying to be a member of your facility or club.

Now look at your place of business. When you walk in, is there lint and dirt on the floor? Are there spots and streaks on the windows and mirrors? Is your retail area unorganized or unprofessional looking? If so, this is absolutely affecting your sales in a negative way.

When you come into your studio, gym, or club, it should be spotless. It should look nice and neat. It should be well lit. It should smell great.

Treat your place like it's a jewelry showcase because it is. Your gym is your gem. Just as somebody probably wouldn't spend $700 to $1,500 in a dirty jewelry store, they also won't spend $700 to $1,500 on a membership to a dirty gym.

Make sure your "showcase" is spotless and represents what you are selling. Something more valuable than anything a jewelry store could ever offer, health, fitness, and longevity.

HAVING FUN YET?

Get free training videos, access to more resources, updates, and upgrades to this book when new versions or editions are released:

Text me

aosmupdates

to

(678) 506-7543

Look Sharp, Be Sharp

Do you remember your impression of Vinny? He was the first jewelry salesperson that we visited. He was unkempt and unprofessional looking. Everything about him looked and felt unsuccessful. In contrast, Giovanni walked, talked, and dressed like success. He's someone you can feel confident taking advice from.

Best selling author and sales trainer, Zig Ziglar once said, "You can't climb the ladder of success dressed like a failure." If you want to be sharp, you have to look sharp. You must have the look of success to be successful in this profession.

I had a salesperson that was really struggling to get his closing percentage up. He was great at booking appointments over the phone and his show up rate was great. When it came to getting the sale, something was off. He was only closing about half of the people who came in as opposed to the 70% to 80% close rate that my other salespeople had. I decided to pay him a visit at his location to see if we could get this figured out.

I told him that when I get to the gym I want him to treat me just like a new prospect for which he had an appointment. I wanted to experience the way that he was handling the sales process from the customer's side of things. He agreed to humor me and I arrived at the gym.

He greeted me at the door with a friendly smile and pleasant personality. I didn't even get two steps into the gym and I think I figured out his problem.

He was wearing a t-shirt and sweatpants. His appearance gave me the impression that he had just gotten out of bed. Actually, his appearance gave me the impression that he *never* got out of bed. I asked him if he was feeling ill.

"No sir. Why do you ask that?" he questioned.

"Because you look like someone that I want to give some Nyquil to and send back to bed. Why are you dressed this way?"

This was a kid was smart and he had a very logical reason for dressing this way. He pointed out that when people are coming in to check out our facility, they are dressed in t-shirts and sweatpants. Since his prospects are dressed this way, he felt that also dressing this way would help them feel more comfortable with him. It was a way for him to develop rapport with the prospect.

Even though your prospect is coming to your facility in sweatpants and a t-shirt, that doesn't mean that is how they normally dress. Your prospects have jobs and probably have to dress better than t-shirts and sweatpants. In addition, very few people are going to spend $1,000 or more with somebody dressed like a $20 bill. I suggested to my salesperson that he change his attire immediately so that he appears to be a lot more professional and successful.

Not only will looking sharp help you with your closing percentages and how your prospect views and perceives you, but it also will help you with your own self-image. If you look good then you will feel good.

Make sure that you are put together for your position. Invest in wardrobe that represents success. Have a nice watch. Wear a nice shirt and pants. Purchase some nice shoes.

Soon after this salesperson started dressing better his closing percentage went up, his income went up, and the happiness he had with his job went up. If you look sharp, you will be sharp. If you represent success you will be a success.

BE SHARPER.

Join me and some of your fellow AOSM readers online at membershipsalesacademy.com. There are hours and hours of video training, interactive lessons, live lectures, and more!

You should join us by going here:

membershipsalesacademy.com

You Can't Win The Race Looking At The Wall

Your mental focus is one of the most important "make or break" factors for being successful in anything that you do. Some would say it's the most important factor. This is especially true in the art of selling memberships. In the same way that if you look sharp, you will be sharp, if you focus on success, you will be successful.

My father in law, "Barefoot" Bob McCreadie, is one of the most successful race car drivers in the history of racing. He has more than five hundred wins in his racing career. Five hundred wins is a lot of wins in anything but let me give you a better perspective of how remarkable of an accomplishment that is in racing.

Richard Petty, known as "The King" is NASCAR's winningest driver at 200 wins. John Force is drag racing's top dog with 126 NHRA wins. Formula One's driver with the most wins is Michael

Schumacher with 91. If you do the math, the combined total of all three of these phenomenal drivers is 417 wins. That's still almost 100 wins away from Barefoot's career total.

My family often goes over to the in laws to visit. One day Bob and I were watching racing on TV. A race car on the track went out of control and hit the inside wall of the racetrack. I wondered what Bob did when his car lost control.

"Bob, have you ever lost control of your car when you were racing?" I asked.

"Of course, plenty of times. Some people would say my car was out of control most of the time," he laughed.

"How did you keep from crashing into the wall then?"

"I kept my eyes on the track," he said, like I should already know this. "When you lose control of your car, you have to look where you want the car to go. If you focus on where you want to go, your hands and feet are going to figure out how to get you there. If you focus on the wall, you'll end up there too. I wanted to win not crash. You can't win races looking at the wall."

When people come to you for help they expect to be led to a solution by a leader not by a loser. In racing, hitting the wall is a failure. Winning the race is success. Focusing on the wall (failure) will only lead you to failure. Focusing on the track (success) will lead you to success. That's where you want to be, so look there. Focus on solutions, look towards success, and you will cross that finish line as a winner.

STAY ON THE WINNING TRACK!

This book is INTERACTIVE - to get free training videos, access to more resources, updates, and upgrades to this book when new versions or editions are released:

Text me

aosmupdates

to

(678) 506-7543

Get Your Mind Right With The Killer Be's

"Killing it" in membership sales is a good thing. It means you are successfully closing your prospects. It means you are helping a lot of people. In order to kill *it*, you have to be a kill*er*.

Being a killer is all about your attitude and your mindset. The mental and emotional state that you let yourself be in while you're in front of a prospect will influence them as much as any of the words that you say.

Here's how you can be a killer and have the right frame of mind for selling memberships. I call them "The Killer Be's."

Killer Be #1: Be Proud

The word salesman or salesperson congers up a negative image for a lot of people. We sometimes think that selling is convincing someone to do something that they don't want to do. It's probably why a lot of us in this business tell ourselves that we "are not a salesperson." If that's your attitude, you are not going to be as successful as you could be.

Imagine that you're the most qualified, the best educated, certified personal trainer out there today. Instead of being proud of it, you tell yourself that you know nothing about training other people. How successful do you think you would be? You won't be. The same thing goes for selling.

I've sold millions and millions of dollars worth of memberships throughout my career. I've helped obese people lose weight. I've helped kids get better grades in school. I've helped people with low self-esteem feel better about themselves. I've helped thousands and thousands of men, women, and children in my life because I sold them a membership. Very few walked into the gym's where I worked and just wrote out a check or gave me their credit card. They had to be sold.

Telling yourself that you are not a salesperson is a self-defeating attitude and will lead to failure.

Don't do that. If you want to be successful in this business, you have to be a successful salesperson. To be a successful salesperson you have to be proud to call yourself a salesperson.

You can and will change people's lives for the better. You will help them become healthier. You will help them develop self-confidence. You will show them the path to feeling better about themselves and increasing their self-esteem. You will help them look better and live longer but first you have to sell them a membership. Be proud of what you have to offer and more importantly is to be proud to be a salesperson.

Killer Be #2: Be Positive

Your alarm is going off in the morning and you've noticed you're a half hour late. You could have sworn you only hit the snooze one time. You jump out of bed and stub your toe on the corner of the bed. Your day is off to a rough start.

This may or may not be news to you but nobody cares. It doesn't matter that you've had a rough start to your morning. Not only does nobody care but also nobody is going to even know unless you complain and tell them. Don't. Take a deep breath and get your Brad Pitt on or your Angelina Jolie on or whatever actor you admire most on. Act as if you had the best morning ever.

When you get to your studio, act confident and act positive. Act as if you're about to have the absolute best day ever and the best night. Act as if you're the best salesperson you have ever heard of or have ever seen.

There is a saying that goes "fake it until you make it." That saying put into the proper context is good advice. Act like everything happening to you is positive and positive things will happen to you. Be positive.

Killer Be #3: Be Passionate

Back in 1996, I went to a sales seminar called *The Competitive Edge* by Anthony Robbins. Robbins became famous through his late night infomercials where he pitched his peak performance program, *Personal Power*.

There are many people who see Robbins as a guy on TV with big teeth and don't realize what a great salesperson he is. This man has sold over 35 million units of his *Personal Power* program from his pitch to late night TV viewers. The man knows how to sell.

The trip to get there took three hours by car but it was worth it. I wasn't the only one who traveled from miles away to attend. Thousands of people from all over the country were there. Some were there for inspiration. Some were there to improve their sales abilities. Some were there to meet the man, Anthony Robbins.

The event was everything that I thought it would be, inspiring, informative, and real world sales techniques that I could use. From time to time during the eight-hour seminar, Robbins asked us to partner up and work with someone near us and participate in different drills and exercises.

One of the exercises that we had to partner up on was a drill where we had to use our body and gestures to communicate with passion. My partner would come up with a mundane product and then I had to explain what it was in the most passionate way possible. He picked a paper clip, not the most exciting product on the market.

As I was to give my passionate presentation about the paper clip, my partner would take notes. He was to look at my face and notice if there were any changes. He was paying attention to my voice, my tone, my inflection, and the rate of my speech. What were my hands and body doing? He had to note it.

"Ready? Go!" my partner shouted.

"Paper clips are so amazing. They hold papers together unlike any other item on the planet. Unlike tape, paper clips are 100% residue free and won't tear your papers when you separate them. Paper clips don't leave holes like staples. Paper clips are amazing at keeping your papers together. Did you know you could also pick locks with a paperclip as well? What an amazingly universal product!"

What was the result of me presenting with passion? I talked faster and louder. My face seemed to brighten up and my eyes got bigger. I smiled. I used hand gestures. My posture seemed to improve and I lean towards him. I made more eye contact.

Try this exercise yourself but do it with your membership in mind. Look in the mirror and communicate the exciting, phenomenal, features, benefits, and solutions that your product provides to your prospect. Note the changes in yourself and practice again.

I recommend that you make sure you are home alone or that you warn the people in your household that you're doing this. You don't want them calling the psychiatric ward about you acting crazy in the mirror.

It is not enough just to have enthusiasm; you must be able to communicate that enthusiasm to your prospect. Your job as a professional is to present the attractive qualities of your membership in the most passionate way possible so that your prospects buy.

Zig Ziglar said, "Selling is a transference of feelings and emotions." The emotion that you are feeling and communicating will transfer to be the emotion that your prospect is feeling. Communicate with passion and they will be passionate about buying from you.

Killer Be #4: Be Caring

Being proud, being positive, and being passionate are critical elements to your success and so is caring about others. People want to do business with someone who cares about them. If you see your prospect just as an opportunity to make money, it will show and you will struggle to find success.

Do you remember the introduction of this book? I thought I had an easy sale, a slam-dunk sale. I was counting the money I was going to make before I even made it. Thinking about how much you're going to make or what you're going to buy when you're trying to sign up a prospect takes the focus off of the prospect.

Look at the prospect as someone that you can help. They have a problem and you have a solution. You can and will help change their life for the better. Become genuinely concerned with helping your prospect achieve their goals and your goals will also be realized.

Caring extends to after the sale as well. Showing that you care after you've made the sale will go a long way to solidifying your reputation as someone that cares about the people you work with. Members will be more likely to refer their friends and family members to you if you are a confident, passionate, and caring salesperson.

FREE BOOK UPDATES AND VIDEO TRAINING

This book is INTERACTIVE - to get free training videos, access to more resources, updates, and upgrades to this book when new versions or editions are released:

Text me

aosmupdates

to

(678) 506-7543

Why People Buy Memberships

When I was eleven years old I started selling and delivering newspapers for my hometown paper, *The Cortland Standard.* I was given about fifty customers or stops as we called them in the business.

Six days a week I would deliver my customer's papers to their doorstep. I collected the money from them once per week and made five cents in profit on each paper that I delivered. That netted me about fifteen dollars per week, which I thought was pretty decent for an eleven-year-old kid.

Monday through Saturday, I would ride my bike to *The Cortland Standard* and pick up my papers for that days delivery. While I was there, I checked in with the delivery manager to get any announcements he may have. This particular day he announced that the paper was having a sales contest to help boost their newspaper subscriptions.

The paper carrier that got the most new subscriptions won fifty whole dollars. That was almost a month's profit for me. This was a contest that I was planning on winning. I thought of all the houses that I passed by that didn't buy newspapers from me. I saw nickel after nickel coming my way. I decided that I was going to stop at every single house on my route and ask them to buy a subscription.

I remember walking up the steps and knocking on the door of that first house on Pendleton Street like it was yesterday. I was nervous as a teenager about to go on his first date. I didn't know who lived there or if they even read the paper. I didn't even know what I was going to say.

I knocked the knuckles of my fist on the door. Knock. Knock. No answer. I knocked harder. Knock! Knock! Knock!

"Who is it," I hear a man grumble from inside.

"My name is Erik from *The Cortland Standard*."

The door opens and standing there is this scruffy looking man in his mid 40's. His white tank top had some kind of orange cheese curl stains on it and barely covered his big ole gut. The sweatpants he had on looked like he had them on yesterday and the day before that *and* the day before that.

"*The Cortland Standard*? What about it?"

"Yes sir. Well, we are having this contest and if I get the most new subscriptions, I win fifty dollars. I was wondering if you wanted to buy a subscription?"

"Nope."

And the door is quickly shut in my face.

"What a jerk," I said to myself. I may have been turned down but I'm not one to be discouraged very easily. I quickly went to the next house and just as quickly I got turned down. Door after door was figuratively and literally shut in my face. I had approached almost all of the people on my route and only had two new subscriptions. Door to door sales is a cold world even for an eleven year old.

Kost Tire was a successful chain of repair shops in my state and their newest location was opening soon on my route. Before I called it a day, I decided to stop in and see if I could sell them a subscription. Even if I landed this account, I was pretty sure that winning the paper's sales contest was out of the question but I was a fighter. If I was going down, I was going down swinging.

The person at the counter was an optimistic, high-energy general manager that had just been given the opportunity of his career, his very own store. This time, my pitch had changed. I had no chance of winning the contest so it was pointless to even mention the stupid contest.

"Sir, my name is Erik and I'm with *The Cortland Standard*. I was riding by and I thought of something you might like. It seems to me that your customers might enjoy reading the newspaper while they wait to get their cars fixed. I'd be happy to stop here everyday and drop off a newspaper for you and your customers, if you would like."

"That's a great idea kid! As a matter of fact, I'll take ten papers everyday and I'll let my customers take them home with them if they want. Can you bring me 10 everyday?"

I couldn't believe it. Did I just sell ten newspapers to one stop? Absofreakinglutely!

"Yes sir!" I exclaimed trying not to jump out of my skin.

"Then you have yourself a deal kid," he said as he shook my hand like his right arm was having a seizure.

Add those ten to my other two and I, in essence, sold twelve new subscriptions. My twelve new subscriptions weren't enough to win the contest but I will never forget the rush. What an amazing feeling it was getting that sale. It's a feeling I work for everyday and twenty-nine years later, it still never gets old.

I eventually grew my subscribers to almost eighty stops before I retired from delivering newspapers at the ripe old age of fourteen. I also never forgot the lesson that I learned that day. A lesson taught to me by the most brutal teacher of all, experience.

People could care less if I was trying to win a contest. To be totally frank about it, they could care less about me. They weren't going to buy a newspaper subscription because of my reasons. It wasn't until I appealed to what was in it for the customer, their reasons that I started to be successful at selling new subscribers.

At the tire place, I didn't talk to the manager about how I wanted to win the contest. I talked to him about how buying newspapers from me would benefit him. Bored customers are unhappy customers. Provide them with a newspaper and they are occupied. So to the manager of the tire place it meant happier customers. Happier customers spend money and bring more customers that spend money. That's why he bought my newspapers.

This principle applies to the art of selling memberships in the same way. Prospects *do not* buy memberships because of your reasons but they *do* buy memberships because of their reasons.

They don't buy because you need to pay a car payment. They don't buy memberships because you're getting married soon. They don't even buy memberships if you're broke and really, really need the commission. Don't ever get this mixed up or you will be broke in this profession.

One of my favorite sales programs of all time is *The Psychology of Selling* by Brian Tracy. Brian Tracy is not only a phenomenal salesperson with real world sales experience but he's also an amazing communicator and teacher. Tracy has books and programs on everything from sales to time management. He has 70 or more different books and programs he's written. If you want to be a highly paid professional, I recommend you put him on your favorites list as well.

In *The Psychology of Selling* he says that whenever you're sitting in front of a prospect always remember the radio station that they are tuned into. It's called W.I.I.–F.M. This stands for (W)hat's (I)n (I)t (F)or (M)e. Tracy goes on to advise that you should picture that question written on your customers forehead at all times because it will remind you that your prospect always wants to know what is in it for them.

Their needs, wants, and motivations is what your prospects care about, not yours. That is why people buy memberships and that is what you need to focus on. This focus will allow you to be able to provide them with a solution for solving their problem. This will help your prospect realize and fulfill their own personal goals. It will also help you fulfill every need and want that you could ever have imagined for yourself.

FREE BOOK UPDATES AND VIDEO TRAINING

This book is INTERACTIVE – to get free training videos, access to more resources, updates, and upgrades to this book when new versions or editions are released:

Text me

aosmupdates

to

(678) 506-7543

The Pleasure And Pain Principle

Think about all of the reasons why someone would want to train at your gym, fitness center, or martial arts studio. What are the specific reasons a prospect will buy a membership from you? They will tell you that they want to lose weight or to get into better shape. Some will say it's to reduce stress. Maybe some have told you that one day, they want to enter a competition. How many more could you come up with or have you heard? Five reasons? Ten reasons? Maybe you could even think of fifteen reasons why they'd want to buy a membership from you.

The answer? The real answer is that there are only two. The only two reasons why your prospect wants a membership is that they are looking to gain future or further pleasure or they want to avoid future or further pain. Remember that they want to gain pleasure and avoid pain. All human beings are motivated by their desire to achieve and avoid these two states.

It was twenty-five years ago; I was fifteen years old at the time. I was already an entrepreneur and had subscriptions to *Success, Inc.,* and *Entrepreneur* magazines. Being a subscriber to these types of magazines got my name on mailing lists for various business and self-improvement types of programs.

One day I received a direct mail letter from a company called Nightingale-Conant. They were marketing an audio cassette program called *Unlimited Power* by peak performance guru, Anthony Robbins. Robbins wasn't the household name that he is now but he was already a best selling author. This program was based on his best selling book of the same name.

The letter claimed that this program would show me, step by step, how to perform at my peak while gaining emotional and financial freedom, attaining leadership and self-confidence, and winning the cooperation of others. That it would give me the knowledge and the courage to achieve my wildest dreams.

But wait, there was more...

I could even try the program free for thirty days and if the program didn't do exactly as the letter had claimed I could return it and owe nothing.

"Whaaaat?" I thought to myself. "This has to be legitimate, they're telling me to use it first. Then, if it doesn't work, I can send it back without having to pay for it."

Nightingale-Conant, you've got yourself a deal. I returned the enclosed order card, in their postage paid envelope, with the "Yes, I want to achieve my wildest dreams" box checked off.

Within a few days the program arrived on my doorstep. I tore into the packaging like a kid opening a Christmas present.

There it was, a shiny black binder with big red letters, *Unlimited Power*. I opened the binder and saw six, silver cassette tapes that looked like jewels glistening in a jewelry showcase. I ran to my bedroom where my tape player was located and got my date with destiny underway.

I didn't leave my room for over seven hours. I listened, I took notes, I rewound the tapes, I listened again, and I followed every drill and exercise Robbins laid out. It was in this program that I was beginning to learn the pleasure and pain principle. If I could appeal to both in someone then I had the power to influence.

Although I was thoroughly enjoying the program, my mother was not. Headphones were not something I had back then and my mother's headphones were off limits. I was driving my mother and everyone else in the house crazy booming Anthony Robbins' voice through my cassette player, over and over. My mother began to worry.

"Erik, what are you listening to? Who is that man with the deep voice," my mother shouted through my locked bedroom door.

"Anthony Robbins, Mom!" I shouted back through the door.

"Who?!"

"Anthony Robbins, Mom! You don't know him!"

"You better not be joining a cult or something like that. Cult's are ..."

I whip the door open and startled her mid sentence.

"Mom, it's not a cult. It's a business program. If you really want to stop hearing it (avoid pain) so you can smoke your cigarettes and drink your coffee in peace (gain pleasure), let me use your headphones."

"A business program? Why the hell would you want to listen to that? It sounds boring but O.K., fine. If want to use my headphones, you can go ahead and use them. Anything so that we don't have to listen to that nonsense," she answered back without seeming to give it any thought.

Us kids were never allowed to use our my Mom's "stuff" because, as she put it, we "ruined everything we touched." Despite the risk of ruin and destruction, she was giving up those headphones like poker chips to a Royal Flush.

The power to influence using pleasure and pain had won her cooperation and I only had the program for a mere seven hours! Nightingale-Conant was right; I really could see my wildest dreams coming true now.

I got the headphones, went back to studying, and fell asleep listening to that program. I studied it until the cassette tapes wore out and promptly sent Nightingale-Conant their $59.99. I'm proud to say that I'm a full-fledged member of the Anthony Robbins "cult" to this day.

Yes, prospects will tell you that they want to lose weight but what they really want is to be more attractive (gain pleasure) and not be treated like a second-class citizen (avoid pain). They will tell you that they want to get in better shape but what they really want is to be able to play with their grandkids (gain pleasure) without having a heart attack and dying (avoid pain). When it comes to the art of selling memberships, understanding the pleasure and pain principle will help you close more sales.

THE PLEASURE OF FREE

VS

THE PAIN OF MISSING OUT

Don't miss out on my free training videos, access to more resources, updates, and upgrades to this book when new versions or editions are released:

Text me

aosmupdates

to

(678) 506-7543

Skills That Pay The Bills

There are three fundamental skills that you will need to master in order to understand the buying motives, wants, and needs of your prospect. These skills are what I call member-oriented skills. The reason I call them member-oriented is because that puts the focus on the prospect. It also creates a positive expectancy that the prospect is going to become a member. The specific skills are questioning, listening, and verifying or "Q,L,V."

The first member-oriented skill that you need to develop mastery in is questioning skills. Asking questions is a fundamental key to being a *good* salesperson. Asking questions that lead to a sale is the key to being a *great* salesperson. I'm going to teach you the specific questions you need to ask in order to lead your prospect to becoming a member.

Knowing the right questions to ask and when to ask them is one of the most important skills to develop in this sales process. You will use these questions to get information from your potential members, to understand their motivations, to clear objections, and to ensure that the person in front of you is actually participating in the art of selling memberships process.

The Most Powerful Question In The Universe

I have two daughters, Kiera and Kylie. At a very young age they learned how to ask the most powerful question in the universe. I'm not saying that to try and impress you with my kid's intelligence. As a matter of fact, if you have kids above the age of two years old, your kids know the most powerful question in the universe as well. I have no idea how they learned it because no sane parent will teach this question to them but they know it and they use it ... frequently. Some of our kids have even learned how to use it with their own little dramatic effect.

You're at the checkout of your local supermarket. You brought along that beautiful little thing you've created called a child. The cashier is scanning your items and you're watching your total go up on the computer screen. Meanwhile, your child is scanning those oh so tempting candy shelves.

"Daddy, can I have a candy bar?"

"No," you reply sternly hoping to shut down any further conversation about it. I have a name for parents who think "no", no matter how you say it, is the end of the conversation. I call them *new* parents. You know who you are.

What does your child ask next? The most powerful question in the universe.

"WHY," she asks.

Why. Behold its power. You can't say yes. You can't say no. It forces you to think. You have to come up with some type of explanation. You are being schooled by the most cunning and naturally skilled salesperson in the game, your child. If there is anyone who is the epitome of the salesperson who can sell "ice to Eskimos", it is your child.

In writing this book, I sought out the help of best selling author, Mike Koenigs. Mike teaches people how to write and publish books. After hearing the story of how he wrote his first book, it inspired me to finally type these letters that you are reading at this very moment.

When Mike was 46 years old, he was diagnosed with Stage 3a cancer. He found himself lying in a bed at Duke University Medical Hospital in North Carolina surrounded by people who were dying. He didn't want to leave this earth without leaving something behind for his wife and young son, Zak. That's the moment Mike decided to write his first book.

With only an hour of strength per day, waking up in a pile of his own hair that had fallen out the night before from chemotherapy, he wrote, published, and promoted his first book. That book became a number one bestseller and he did it from his hospital bed using his iPhone.

In learning how to write my book Mike taught me that the first thing I need to do is figure out my "Big Why." Why did I want to write a book? Why would anyone buy it?

In Mike's case his "Big Why" was obvious to him. There was a chance he was going to die soon. He wanted to leave a message and a legacy for his young son to follow and be inspired by. He also wanted to create something that could produce an income for his family long after he passed away.

The great news is, Mike didn't die. Not only did he not die but also he went on to write seven best selling books and has taught over five hundred people to do the same. I'm one of them.

The "Big Why" as Mike calls it has to do with understanding and motivation. Our kids ask us why to get an explanation (and to wear us down) of why we say "no" to candy bars. Mike asked himself why to get the motivation to overcome seemingly insurmountable odds.

In the art of selling memberships you ask why for the same reasons. When you ask your prospect why, their mental computer will search for and come up with an answer. Those answers help you get a better understanding of your prospects motivation for doing what they are doing.

There are so many gyms, clubs, and studios out there, probably ten or more within a twenty-five mile radius of yours. Why did they come to your gym? Why should they become a member?

Two thirds of the America's population is fat, out of shape, and obese. Why does your prospect want to be different?

The more "whys" that you ask, the deeper the understanding you will have of your prospect. Humor me for a moment and let me demonstrate this by asking you why you bought this book. Why did you?

You may answer, "Because I want to be a better salesperson."

Why do you want to be a better salesperson?

Your next answer may be, "because I want to make more money."

Why do you want to make more money?

"Because I want to buy a nice car."

Why do you want a nice car?

"Because a nice car will attract women."

Why do you want to attract women?

"Because I want sex!"

You see? Your ultimate motivation for buying my book is sex. Something that I would have never understood about you until I asked you "why?!"

This might be an example that is exaggerated, although I'm not sure it's exaggerated all that much. You get my point.

In asking your prospect why, you're getting a deeper and better understanding of them and their motivations. In trying to understand them better, you will present yourself as someone who actually cares about them and you'll be better at selling them a membership that solves their problem.

Later in this book I'm going to teach you the specific questions to ask that will uncover your prospect's motivation and eliminate their objections at the same time.

Now That You've Asked, It's Time To Listen

The second skill that you need to master in the art of selling memberships is the skill of listening. Listening is not just hearing. Hearing is a physical capability. Listening requires skill and practice. By listening, I mean that you understand what your prospective member is saying to you.

I have three tips that will help you become a better listener.

<u>**Tip #1**</u>

Focus on what your prospect is saying now not on what you are going to say next. If you are thinking about what you're going to say next, it's almost impossible to think about what your prospect is saying now. Stay tuned into what they are saying first.

Tip #2

Give yourself time to process what they just said. You don't need to fill every second with conversation. That's called being annoying. Don't be that person. By taking a moment to process what they are saying, you will be more relaxed and better able to lead your prospect to buying a membership.

Tip #3

Take notes of everything that your prospect is saying. By taking notes you are putting additional thought into evaluating and processing what your prospect is saying. You are also demonstrating to your prospect that you value what they are saying.

There may also be a point at the close where you have to show the prospect what they said. One of my old sales managers used to always say, "buyers are liars." If that's true, they will be less likely to lie when their own words are visible on paper. Writing down what your prospect says is also a form of verifying, which you will learn about next.

Verifying

The final skill that is fundamental to your success in the art of selling memberships is a skill called verifying. Verifying is the verbal and written confirmation that you and your prospect understand each other. It demonstrates that you are listening to your prospect. It will also help you build trust that you will need when you make the recommendation to become a member.

Developing and mastering these three member-oriented skills will allow you to ask the right questions, hear and understand what your prospect is saying, and most importantly offer a solution that sells a membership. Q, L, V, is the foundation and backbone of the art of selling memberships.

KEEP YOUR SKILLS ON POINT

Join me and some of your fellow AOSM readers online at membershipsalesacademy.com. There are hours and hours of video training, interactive lessons, live lectures, and more!

You should join us by going here:

membershipsalesacademy.com

The New Blood Is The Lifeblood: Generating Sales Leads

Before you can sell a membership, you have to have someone interested in buying. A martial arts studio, gym, fitness center, or club lives and dies by the amount of new members it can generate.

People are going to quit and they are going to quit every month. They might have to move away from the area. They might get injured at work and can no longer train. Whatever their reasons are doesn't matter. Your business needs to constantly bring in new people. This is especially true if you are working on one hundred percent commission. The new blood is the lifeblood.

In addition to the new leads that your company provides, if any, you are going to have to come up with your own. I say "if any" because if you're just starting out in the art of selling memberships, do not put much weight on the leads from the company. They are probably crappy, old leads that the last new guy couldn't close from months ago.

The fresh, new leads are going to the top salesperson and they should. The new leads are gold to the company and they need to go to the person that has proven that they can close sales.

You are an unproven, wannabe at this point. Gold goes to the winners, the closers. Prove yourself as a closer and you will get those fresh, new leads. Until then, you are probably going to be on your own for new prospects.

Doing the work that it takes to generate leads isn't always fun. It's hard work to be honest. Reframe what you're doing from getting a lead to being a Superhero. Superheroes don't like fighting bad guys, they like saving people. Super Hero salespeople may not like going after and getting leads but they do like helping people.

Remind yourself that every lead could be a life that you save by showing the way to better health, a better self-image, or a better way to deal with the everyday stress that they go through.

Generating leads has more to do with marketing than it does selling. There are many good books and programs on the market for generating leads. However, I'm not going to leave you hanging like that. Subscribe to my YouTube channel for the newest, most up-to-date membership marketing ideas, tips, and strategies. youtube.com/erikcharlesrussell

SIGN UP FOR YOUR FREE BOOK UPDATES NOW

Get free training videos, access to more resources, updates, and upgrades to this book when new versions or editions are released:

Text me

aosmupdates

to

(678) 506-7543

Handle With Care: The Four Types Of Leads And How To Deal With Them

There are four types of leads that you will get in this business. Leads through the telephone, leads through social media or the internet, leads through walk-ins, and leads from face-to-face contact like trade shows, fairs, parties, and just going about your everyday life.

In general you have less than one minute to make a good first impression with someone. Remember what we learned previously in this book. You need to be professional looking with a pleasing personality and have a positive mental attitude.

Believe it or not but most people have apprehensions about getting in shape and losing weight. They also have apprehensions about spending their money with someone they aren't comfortable with. Even if you're prospect approached you, they will have apprehensions about buying a membership from you. It's important that you make them feel comfortable.

Your prospect needs to feel like you are going to be a fresh new solution to what is probably an old problem for them.

There is a very good possibility that they've tried to lose weight or working out in the past and have failed. Failing isn't fun and getting back up and trying again can be scary for most people. They don't want to fail again so they're looking for reasons to say no. Not starting is the easiest way to avoid failing.

If they are brand new to working out, getting in shape, or losing weight, your communications need to be about how beginner friendly you are. Let your prospect know that "new people" are your expertise. That is why you are so successful in the first place. You are good at helping people with little or no experience succeed at accomplishing their goals. Communicate to your prospective member that your program has succeeded for many people who were previously in the same position that they are in now.

Telephone Mastery

If new blood is the lifeblood of your business, then the telephone is the lifeline. Almost every prospect you are going to deal with will have some contact via the telephone. If you met them in person, you will have to call and confirm or make an appointment over the phone. You may have a lead that contacted you through social media and you need to follow up with them, you will do that on the phone. Your success or failure in utilizing the telephone will directly impact your income and your success in the art of selling memberships. It's extremely important to master this tool and make people feel at ease over the phone.

Because almost every situation will eventually lead back to the phone, I'm going to spend the most time talking about telephone mastery. Telephone mastery is about having an abundant proficiency in utilizing the telephone for gaining new appointments. The principles that apply to mastering the telephone are universal. What I mean is that these principles will also apply to handling walk-ins, the Internet, and the face-to-face contacts.

When speaking to someone, how you say something is just as important if not more important than what you say. The quality of your voice, its tone, and the rate of your speech all affect the impression that you give your prospect. Keep in mind the ways that we communicate with passion that was covered in this book previously. They apply here.

Phone tip:

Something that I used to do before I made phone calls was listening to music that got me pumped up. I'd put my headphones on, crank up the tunes, and literally dance around like a Native American medicine man for ten minutes or so. I wanted to be in a good mood and have a high energy level. Something Anthony Robbins calls "getting into your peak state." Music helped me do that. What can you do to put yourself in a peak performance state? Figure it out and do it right before you make calls.

When the phone rings, the person on the other end is going to ask you, if not first thing then second thing, "how much is it to join." There is a reason that people ask you how much it is to train and it has nothing to do with the price. The reason is that they have no idea what else to ask. What they're trying to do is take something they know about, money, and relate it to something they know nothing about, working out, losing weight, etc.

When the prospect is on the other end of the phone and they ask you how much it costs, you have to answer them. I've heard all kinds of flowery sales techniques to dance around this type of question. If you don't answer this question directly you're going to come across as a shady con artist. That is obviously not a good first impression.

Now, when I say, "answer the question", I don't mean quote your prices. You never, ever quote a price over the phone. You cannot sell a membership over the phone. There is absolutely no need to give them a price if they are not ready to buy.

In fact, if you're quoting people prices over the phone you're actually doing them a disservice. You're also doing your business a disservice. What you're telling them is that there is no benefit to choosing you over the competition, other than price. If you get into this price battle with your competition it will affect your income in a negative way. Leave the price battles to Wal-mart and K-mart, you should not be competing based on price.

What you should be doing is communicating your value based on the quality of your program, the quality of your instructors, cleanliness of your club, and in the results that you get for people. Telling your prospect over the phone that your program is as low as $19.95 per month does not do that.

Now, like I said, you do have to answer the question. Simply let them know that the price of joining really depends on the program they select. Then immediately ask them a question to get control of the conversation and lead the prospect to an appointment. Let's take a look at how a conversation might go to get a better idea of what I'm talking about and how to work this.

Prospect:

"Hi, yeah, I was calling to see how much it is to join."

You:

"Thank you for your interest. The price of your membership here is going to depend on the program that you choose. We have quite a few options. Have you ever trained before/been a member of a gym before or is this something new for you?"

You answered the prospects question with something that makes sense and is true. You've told them that the price of their membership depends on the program that they select. Unless you only have one program to choose from, which I strongly discourage, you're being honest with them. You've also told the prospect that there are different programs and different programs usually have different prices.

Asking a question at the end seems to help you narrow down the choice of programs. You are asking if they are new or experienced. In the prospects mind, that's two different programs right there. Questions also control the conversation and you are getting the conversation back under your control. You need to be in control to lead your prospect to an appointment.

Imagine for a moment that you're selling cars. You're sitting at your desk and the phone rings. You answer the phone and it's a prospective customer looking for a new car.

Prospect:

"Hi, yeah, I'm looking to get a new car. How much are they?"

You:

"New cars are $35,000. When can you come in a buy one?"

It sounds ridiculous doesn't it? That's because quoting prices over the phone is ridiculous. Don't do it with your memberships. A car customer wouldn't necessarily ask this over the phone because they expect the type of vehicle, the amount of options, etc to determine the price. They don't expect that with a membership because they don't know anything about them. You don't know what they want or need at this point so there is no need to be giving them a price. If you do, your ability to appointment close goes down which ultimately affects your income in a negative way. You can't sell someone a membership who doesn't make an appointment. Let's continue our conversation with our prospective member.

Prospect:

"Oh, I'm new at this. I've never joined a gym before in my life."

You:

"Ok, great. Do not worry at all. We are very beginner friendly. That's one of the reasons why we've been in business so long. We're good at helping new people with little or no experience get great results in a safe and healthy way. What is the main reason that you're calling? What is the goal you are looking to accomplish by becoming a member?"

This answer sets them at ease. You are telling them directly not to worry. Then you reinforce your statement by saying that you welcome beginners by being beginner friendly. Lastly, you add social proof to what you're saying by commenting about all of the years that you've been in business. Obviously your club wouldn't still be in business if you weren't good with helping out beginners. Then you tell them why, you get results in a safe and healthy way.

You are starting to make them feel comfortable with you. The next thing you do is, ask another question. This maintains your control of the conversation and the type of question moves you to discussing their actual goal. The prospect talking about themselves is what the art of selling memberships is all about. Back to our conversation with our prospective member.

Prospect:

"I'm looking to lose weight."

You:

"Very good. That's actually the number reason why people become members here, to lose weight and get in shape, so you've called the right place. Can I ask your name?"

Prospect:

"It's Judy."

You:

"Ok, Judy. What I normally do is have you come in and try out our club/program for free. I'll talk to you a little bit more about your goals and some ways that we can achieve them when you come in.

This free session gives me the opportunity to see where you're at and help me make the best program recommendation that I can. The free session also allows you to try us out without any obligation and see if you like it. Let's talk about when you're available to come in for your free session. Do you work days or nights?"

Asking if they work days or nights is an easy way of finding out if they have a job or not. It's a way of qualifying your prospect. If they have a job proceed with booking the appointment. We'll deal with the unemployed in a moment.

Prospect:

"I work days."

You:

"Ok great. I have an opening at 5:30 pm today. Does that work for you?"

Prospect:

"Yes."

Be sure to get their phone number so that you can confirm the appointment later, if necessary. You will also need it to follow up if they miss their scheduled appointment.

Make sure they also understand where you are located and how to get there. I've had too many occasions where I spent the money and time getting the prospect to call and book an appointment only to have them show up at a competing gym! Make sure that they know how to get to you, especially if they have to drive by competitors to get to you.

If your prospect says they are not working, you need more information. The last thing you want to do is put time and energy into someone who ultimately won't be able to buy a membership because they have no source of income. Let's have that conversation with our prospect.

Prospect:

"I'm not working right now."

You:

"Ok. Judy, let me ask you, if you liked a program we have for you here and wanted to continue, how would you pay for it?"

You'll get various answers. Sometimes they are a stay at home parent and the other parent will be paying. Sometimes they are in college and Mom or Dad is footing the bill. If that's the case, confirm that they can make the buying decision or arrange to have the decision maker be present at the appointment as well.

Prospect:

"Oh my husband pays for everything."

You:

"Ok, sounds like a good deal. Should we have him come with you or can you decide about the membership without him?"

When you get your answer, book the appointment accordingly. If she says that her husband has to be there, then you have to book an appointment that they both can make. If she says that she can make the buying decision without him then go ahead and book the appointment without him.

If they have no job and no way of paying for a membership, you need to tell them to give you a call when they have their finances in order. Setting appointments with people who do not have the ability to pay is a big time waster. Following this process will help you eliminate that altogether.

Walk-In Mastery

Mastering the walk-in is very similar, in terms of what you say, to mastering the telephone. Again, your prospect is probably going to lead with the price question. You use the technique here that I detailed previously in the telephone mastery section when they ask for it. Sometimes you will get a prospect that feels like they deserve to hear the price because they are physically in your gym. Do not let that distract you from getting into a discussion about their goals.

Prospect:

"I know what I want and how to workout. I'm just looking for the cheapest membership price in town."

You:

"Sir, let me ask you this. If price is your only concern then why did you come into the club? You obviously are looking for certain things in a facility and I can appreciate that. Take a look around with me and let me know if we have what you're looking for. We can talk a little bit about your fitness goals and what you're trying to accomplish. That will help me narrow down some membership options. Does that work for you?"

As you're taking them around ask them about their goals. Use a shortened version of the motivation and commitment questioning process I detail later in the book.

Face-To-Face Mastery

In going about your everyday life you will come into contact with a lot of people. More than you probably realize. Mastering the face-to-face opportunity means taking someone from a chance encounter from outside of your place of business and getting their contact information and/or an appointment.

Many times the question comes up, "What do you do for a living?" If your answer is boring, "I'm a Program Director for a health club," you will get a boring response and probably nothing more.

If your answer is interesting, people will be more interested. A more interesting answer would be, "I take people from where they are right now, which is usually tired, a little overweight, and defeated at the end of the day to feeling great, looking dead sexy/like a beast, and crushing their day. Everyday. Sounds like fun right?"

The technical term in selling for this is an elevator speech. You craft your elevator speech so that in 60 seconds or less, about the same time that it takes to ride an elevator, you have a potential prospect interested in wanting to hear more from you. Use the elevator speech I have above or come up with a couple on your own.

The Three Feet Rule

The three feet rule is simply that anybody who comes within three feet of your proximity hears your elevator speech. As one of my business mentors, Barry VanOver likes to say, "now, don't hear what I'm not saying." I'm not saying you run up and ambush every person within three feet of you. Make a point to make eye contact with people. Smile when you see someone. If they don't ask what you do for a living, ask them what they do for a living. Look for clues and opportunities to get a conversation going with anyone who comes within three feet of you.

Internet, Email, Social Media Mastery

I put the Internet, email, and social media together because I treat all digital correspondence the same.

Your goal is to sell a membership. That is not something you can do effectively through your smartphone, tablet, or computer. You need their contact information so that you can call them.

Getting your prospects contact information is similar to how you handle all of your other opportunities for getting leads. You make them feel comfortable with you, give them social proof, and ask them a question.

Email from a prospect:

"I'm interested in joining your gym and was wondering how much it was to join. Thanks."

Your reply back:

"Hi (use their name),

Thank you for your interest in training at Name Fitness. The price of your membership depends on the program that you choose. Right now we are offering a free trial on all of our programs so that you can see what you like and then pick the best option for you. Have you ever trained before or is this something new for you? Better yet, how about I give you a call and we can figure some of this out over the phone? Message me your phone number and best time to call and I will be in touch with you. Thanks again for your interest. I'm looking forward to working with you.

All the best,

Erik"

This correspondence keeps the focus on the prospect. "Your membership", "you choose", and "best option for you", gives them the feeling of being in control of the situation. They didn't give you their number initially because they were nervous for one reason or another and want to maintain control of the conversation. This response gets you in control of the conversation and at the same time doesn't make the prospect feel like they have lost control.

When the prospect replies with their contact information follow the technique for booking the appointment in the telephone mastery section.

DID YOU SIGN UP FOR YOUR FREE BOOK UPDATES?

To get your free updates:

Text me

aosmupdates

to

(678) 506-7543

Discovering What Your Prospects Really Want

Imagine being able to sell without encountering any resistance to the sales process whatsoever. Your prospect signs on the dotted line, pays for their membership, and loves you for "letting" them become a member. It sounds awesome, doesn't it? It is.

The reason it was so easy for you to sign them up was because you learned your prospect's true motivations and offered them a membership that they need and want. In order to get to the bottom of what is really motivating them you have to ask them questions.

The questions that I'm about to teach you are actually going to do three things for you. First, they will as promised reveal what your prospects really want. By asking these questions you will have a deeper understanding for the reasons that they walked into your gym, school, or fitness center in the first place.

Second, these questions will help you eliminate your prospects objections before they even have them. Asking your prospect about the objections and eliminating them up front will stop the objection from coming up when you're talking about the price at the end. It allows you to have an honest and open discussion about their motivations when your prospect is the most willing to be honest with you, before they know the price. If you have not fully satisfied their objections prior to talking about the cost of the membership, you will be fighting an uphill battle trying to get the honest reason why they are telling you no at the close.

And third, these questions will help you retain your prospect as a happy member for a long time to come. Overcoming the objections at the end isn't impossible and if you're a well-schooled salesperson you can do it. The problem with that is you may come across as a cheesy con man and send your new member home with buyer's remorse.

Buyer's remorse is when the buyer feels guilty about the purchase after they have made it. We've all experienced it at some point or another after a purchase that we've made. You think to yourself that you wish you had taken more time to think about your purchase before making it. The salesperson should have helped you think it through better. It leaves a bad taste in your mouth so to speak and it's very bad for future business.

In this business, people can legally cancel their contract for a variety of reasons. If they live past a certain number of miles from your gym, they can cancel. If they bring you a doctor's note saying they can't participate, they can cancel. In my state, New York, they can cancel for any reason whatsoever up to three days after signing and you also have to refund them their down payment. Send them home with buyer's remorse and your cancellations are going to be higher than they need to be.

Follow the art of selling memberships and you will encounter less resistance from your prospect in signing up, they will be happier for becoming a member, and your buyer's remorse cancellations will be virtually zero. I've used it to sell millions and millions of dollars worth of memberships to a lot of happy customers and clients.

DO YOU WANT FREE BOOK UPDATES AND VIDEO TRAINING?

This book is INTERACTIVE – to get free training videos, access to more resources, updates, and upgrades to this book when new versions or editions are released:

Text me

aosmupdates

to

(678) 506-7543

The Four Objections That Every Prospect Has

There are a lot of books on overcoming sales objections. You might think that with so many books out there then there must be a lot of objections that a prospect could come up with. While this is true in a general sense, our business, the business of selling memberships, there are only four objections that you are going to encounter.

The first objection we hear is, "The location is a little far for me to travel or I don't have transportation or the weather is bad. Let me get back to you tomorrow."

Objection number two is, "You know my schedule is pretty crazy. I'll know by the end of this week what my schedule is. Let me see if I have the time to commit and then we'll go from there."

The third objection is based on their commitment. You'll hear, "You know, I don't think I'm going to be able to stick with it and I have a treadmill in my basement. Let me think about it and I'll get right back to you."

The final objection you're going to encounter is the significant other. "I've got to talk to my wife before I can sign up. Let me talk to her and if she's good with it, I'll join."

If you notice, which I'm sure you did, money is not an objection. People do not say no to you because they can't afford it. They are saying no to you because you are not meeting their needs and they are afraid to commit.

In purchasing your membership they are committing to a time period whereby they are going to have to put in work to achieve the desired results. Both of those things are scary for a lot of people. Especially people who have failed at achieving a goal like losing weight in the past.

The reason that money is not an objection is because there are many ways that you can show your prospect how they can afford your membership. If they are motivated to do it, they will find a way, or make a way to fit your monthly membership into their budget. It's not really a matter of not being able to afford it; it's a matter of making some changes.

Your prospect may need to alter their diet. You may have to explain to them that stopping at Starbucks every morning or even every other morning is going to have to stop. They might have to cut back on the number of times that they go out to eat. Maybe they are going to have to stay in on Saturday nights instead of going to the local bars.

If you use the questions that I'm about to teach you to handle these four objections, your prospect will make these changes in their spending habits willingly and happily. If they truly cannot afford your membership, that is not an objection, that is a circumstance. If that is the case then you need to move on to someone who is in a better circumstance to afford the help that you are offering.

Another important note to make here before we get into the nuts and bolts, so to speak, is the order in which to handle this process. It's imperative that you follow this process exactly as I'm laying it out. By guiding your prospect through this process as I show it, you are taking the prospect on an emotional journey that is very powerful. I liken it to a good movie.

Think about your favorite movie. In the beginning you learn a little bit about the main character. You learn about their background, their style, and their way of being who they are. Then the main character goes through some sort of struggle and has to face an obstacle. Just when the main character looks like they are going to fail, they come through and succeed. In the end, they live happily ever after. You loved the movie and feel great after you watched it.

Your prospect is going to participate in that same emotional journey in the art of selling memberships. Your prospect is the main character and you are the director. Your prospect will get a solution to their problem, you will make a lot of money, and you both will live happily ever after.

FREE BOOK UPDATES AND VIDEO TRAINING

This book is INTERACTIVE - to get free training videos, access to more resources, updates, and upgrades to this book when new versions or editions are released:

Text me

aosmupdates

to

(678) 506-7543

Eliminating Objections Before Your Prospect Presents Them

In our conversations with the prospect, I'm going to focus on the goal of weight loss. Weight loss, also referred to as getting into shape by your prospect, is by far the number one reason people seek out a personal trainer, coach, fitness center, or club. It's also your biggest market as approximately 2/3 of the U.S. population is overweight or obese.

When you understand this sales process you can substitute any goal in the place of weight loss. Maybe you run a martial arts school and discipline is what your prospect is looking for. Your prospect might have a high stress job and they are looking for something to help reduce the effects of that stress on their health. The list goes on but they are all handled the same way, using the same sales process. By questioning, by listening, and by verifying at each objection.

Remember to take notes and write down what your prospect's answers are. Write the answers down on a piece of paper so that your prospect can see it.

Also get a definitive "yes" or "no" answer from your prospects. No "maybes". No "I think so." No vagueness whatsoever. When they are vague, you are assuming that they are giving you the affirmative. At the end when it's time to buy you will see that the prospect will remind you that they didn't say, "yes" just to get out of making a decision. If they say "yes" you can continue with the sales process. If they say "no" at any point then you cannot sell them a membership without clearing that "no". Got it? All right, let's sell some memberships.

Objection #1: Location, Transportation, and Weather

In order to take advantage of the benefits of becoming a member of your facility, your prospect has to be able to get there. Do not assume that just because they made it to their appointment or walked in the door that they can get to your place regularly from wherever they live or work.

You must get them to agree that getting to your location isn't a problem. That goes not only for the distance that they have to travel to get to you but it also goes for the weather conditions.

If you live in sunny San Diego, CA then the weather probably isn't going to be much of an issue. I live in Watertown, NY and it can be cold and blustery quite a bit. When it's cold and blustery, people are less likely to leave their warm home, get in their car, come to the gym, and work their butts off. When they aren't at the gym, they are getting out of their routine, and the idea of cancelling their membership slowly starts to creep into their mind.

Maybe they are close enough to walk to the gym. That's great but don't assume they will do it. Make them confirm that they will be able to get to you be it hell or high water. By any means necessary through driving, biking, or walking.

Q, L, V, for Location, Transportation, and Weather:

You:

"I noticed from your application that you live about X miles from here. How do you plan on getting here if we can put together a workout program for you?"

Prospect:

"I have a car. I'll be driving" or "I can ride my bike" or "I'll walk."

You:

"Are we located conveniently enough for you to be able to make it in at least a couple of times per week?"

If they give you an affirmative answer, you write it down on your notes. *"Can get here a couple of times per week even if has to walk"* is something I might write down. Whatever they say, you write their words on your paper. Remember that in verifying their answer, they need to see that you are writing down their words. This will remind them at the close of the sale that they already told you that they could get to your place.

Once you have confirmed that they have the transportation to get to you. Ask them about the change in the weather.

You:

"As you know Mrs. Prospect, we get some snow around here from time to time. Are you going to be able to get to us even if the weather is a bit snowy?"

Prospect:

"I will get here no matter what. Rain, sleet, or snow. I'll be here."

Write it down.

If the response is to the negative, you simply cannot move on in the sales process. How are you going to ethically sell someone a membership that can't even get to you? I will say though, if your prospect has a friend that already comes to the gym, I would call that friend and find out if they could ride together. If yes, sell them a membership. If not, thank the prospect for being interested but if they can't get to you then you cannot help them.

Objection #2: Time and Schedule

I consider this objection one of the most ridiculous objections of them all. In the day and age of the smartphone, who doesn't know their schedule? If your prospect really didn't have the time, why are they sitting in front of you in the first place? The truth is that everybody has the time to workout a few times per week.

Time and schedule are the easiest objections to overcome in the beginning but a major pain in the ass if you try to close them after you've talked price. Go over price before you clear this one and you'll hear, "I've got to check my schedule (at work, with my wife, with my buddies, etc, etc) and I'll get back to you." Now, you don't know whether it's really their schedule that is the issue or if it's something else.

Remember what my old sales manager said? That's right. Buyers are liars. They will tell you that it's their schedule they need to check when the reality might be that they just don't want to make a decision. They will tell you that they don't think that they have the time when the reality is your buyer feels like they lack the ability to follow through on things.

We want to believe that most people are honest. I believe that most people are honest ... until it comes time to part with their money. Then the harsh reality is this, buyers *are* liars. My old sales manager was right. Ask them to pay for something and you'll get all kinds of reasons why they can't do it.

You control the moment that your prospect goes from a prospect to a buyer. Follow my process and clear the time and schedule objection in the beginning, when they are still a prospect. That is when they will be honest with you. Let me be your teacher on this one and do not learn it through experience. It's a very painful lesson to learn through experience. In the end, you're going to find that I'm right anyway. The good news is that the time and schedule objection is the easiest to clear when you follow the art of selling memberships.

Q, L, V, for Time and Schedule

If you are talking to your prospect about specific classes they need to attend, ask them this:

You:

"Mr. Prospect, we run our classes at X times during the day, 4 days per week. Do those times fit your schedule?"

If you're selling a facility membership where they can come and go at anytime you are open, phrase it like this:

You:

"Mr. Prospect we are open from 5 am to 10 pm everyday. Are you going to be able to get in here a few times per week between those hours?"

Prospect:

"Yes, I can."

Write it down. I may write something like "*class time fit his schedule*" or "*can get here a few times per week during our normal business hours.*"

Objection #3: Motivation and Commitment

This is the most important step in the sales process. People will not come right out with their true reasons for being in front of you, you must uncover them through a few different questions. Sometimes they have never even expressed or talked about their true motivations with anyone.

Those motivations and feelings, when exposed, can be very emotional for your prospect. There have been numerous occasions where I've had a prospect shed tears during our conversations. This will happen in front of you too. Do not let that get you off track. You have to uncover and understand these emotional reasons. This will not only help you close the sale but it will also help you to keep them motivated and retain them as a member down the road. Be a leader and lead them to a solution for their pain. That solution is getting in better shape, losing weight, etc.

Q, L, V, for Motivation and Commitment

You:

"Now Mr. Prospect, we talked a little bit about your goal is weight loss. You told me/wrote down on your application that losing weight is important to you. How much weight are you interested in losing?"

This gives us a specific goal to track, measure, and make actionable. It also makes their idea of losing weight tangible. Wanting to lose weight is vague. Wanting to lose 15 to 20 pounds is tangible.

Prospect:

"I'm looking to lose 15 to 20 pounds."

You:

"Excellent. Sounds like you have thought about this goal for a while to have a specific number like that. How long have you been thinking about losing weight?"

Prospect:

"About a year now."

This puts time into context here. The truth is your prospect has probably been thinking about this goal for a while, months and maybe even years. If they've been overweight for a year or more, don't let them tell you that they lack commitment!

They have been unhealthy, fat, and feeling like crap for a year or more. That takes commitment. You're going to get them looking and feeling better than ever before. Tell them to commit to being healthy and feeling good for as long as they have been unhealthy and feeling like crap. Then they can go back to being unhealthy, fat, and feeling like crap if they really want to.

At the end of this sales process if your prospect still says, "I need to think about it," you can remind them that they've already thought about it. Now is the time to make a decision and take the action required to accomplish their goals. They have created a lot of positive momentum towards that by already thinking, then by calling or emailing, and now by actually coming to the gym. Your prospect needs to keep that momentum going by becoming a member today, right now. Back to our conversation.

You:

"Have you ever lost or tried to lose this kind of weight in the past?"

Prospect:

"Yes, I have."

You:

"What are some of the methods that you've tried in the past?"

Prospect:

"Dieting."

You:

"What else have you tried?"

Prospect:

"Weight loss pills."

You:

"What else?"

Prospect:

"Treadmill in my basement."

You:

"Anything else?"

Almost everyone that will come to your studio will have attempted to accomplish their goal in the past. Make sure that you have your prospect list every single thing that they have tried in the past. The more that they have tried and failed the better.

Everything that they list off to you is just a future objection that has been eliminated.

Your prospect might say at the close, "I think I'll try working out at home instead." It's now very easy for you to remind them that doing it on their own doesn't and hasn't worked for them. It's now time to let someone help. It's time to become a member but first we have to get them to the close. Our conversation continues.

You:

"Mr. Prospect why do you think that none of those things you've tried, have worked in the past?"

Prospect:

"I couldn't stay motivated." "I got bored." "I didn't see any results."

When it's time to close the sale you are going to remind them what they told you about failing. If they said that boredom was the reason that they failed, then you're going to show them how your plan is to change the routine up monthly to keep it fresh and exciting. If they say that they couldn't stay motivated, you're going to explain how having exciting goals and working with a certified personal trainer will keep them inspired. Be prepared to remind them and address whatever their reason for failing in the past was. If you don't, your prospect may feel like this is just one more thing that they will fail at and never sign up.

Now we need to get into their feelings about their goal. This is where our conversation gets interesting.

You:

"Mr. Prospect, let's imagine for a minute that you have accomplished this glorious goal of losing twenty pounds. How do you think you will feel?"

Prospect:

"I think I'll feel great!"

Great is not an answer that works. It's too vague, just like losing weight is too vague. You need them to be specific. Making them be specific takes it from vague to tangible. The more they think about the feeling of being twenty pounds lighter the more emotionally attached they become to that goal. The more emotionally attached they are, the more likely they are going to want to accomplish it. The more they want to accomplish it, the more likely they are to become a member and stay a member. So let's get specific in our conversation.

You:

"When you say great, what do you mean? You're 20 pounds lighter right now. How do you feel and see yourself physically? Do you have a six-pack set of abs? Are you playing with your grandchildren without getting tired? Are you seeing yourself being happier? What is it that you mean by great when you say you'd feel great being twenty pounds lighter?"

Prospect:

"Yes by great I mean, I feel good about myself."

You:

"So when you're looking in the mirror, you're seeing something that you're proud of? Knowing that you're 20 pounds lighter has improved your self esteem and your self image?"

Prospect:

"Yes, I guess you could say that."

You:

"Can you actually say that? Will being twenty pounds lighter and accomplishing this goal really make you feel great about yourself?"

Prospect:

"Yes."

You:

"How will that impact and improve your life outside of the gym? Will feeling great and looking great improve your personal life or relationship?"

Prospect:

"Yes, I think it would."

You:

"Why? How so?"

Prospect:

"I think it will help feel more attractive to others."

You:

"Being more attractive to others means what? I don't mean to put words in your mouth but does that mean that you're going on more dates? Does that mean you're getting more positive attention from your wife?"

Ask the question that's appropriate to the prospect that you're dealing with.

Prospect:

"Ha-ha. Yeah, I'd like to have a few more dates."

You:

"Ok, great. So losing this weight is going to help you be more attractive and get more dates, maybe even help you find a soul mate or at least help you have more fun finding a soulmate! What do you think being more attractive is going to do for you mentally and emotionally? Do you think you'll be happier, more confident, less stressed? How do you feel mentally and emotionally about being twenty pounds lighter?"

Prospect:

"Well, I'm definitely going to feel more confident about myself and that makes me happy."

You:

"What other positive impacts do you think this will have on your life? How will this affect your professional life, your job, if you're a more confident person?"

Prospect:

"It will probably help with my motivation at work. Help me do a better job."

You:

"Mr. Prospect, confidence at your job is one of the best ways to not only stay motivated at work but to enjoy what you're doing more. If you enjoy it more, you will do better at it. Next thing you know, you're getting that promotion you know you want."

What you're doing is helping your prospect make an emotional attachment to accomplishing their goal of losing that twenty pounds. You're helping them feel and experience the benefits of being twenty pounds lighter now. This is moving your prospect towards the pleasure part of the Pleasure and Pain Principle that we covered earlier in the book.

What are some other moving towards pleasure feelings they could have?

Getting in shape means that I can breathe better. When I look in the mirror, I see that six pack on my abs.

Having an outlet for my stress will make me a happier person. I will have more friends.

Improving my discipline will allow me to make better decisions in life. It will give me better focus on what I'm trying to accomplish.

What are some moving towards pleasure feelings that you can come up with?

Now that we've established the prospect's moving towards pleasure motivations, the next thing that we need to do is establish the prospect's moving away from pain motivation. This is the state that they are currently experiencing and more than likely the biggest motivator for your prospect. Most people will do more to avoid pain than they will to gain pleasure so this is an important part. Let's talk with our prospect about why it's painful for them to be in the position they are in now (twenty pounds overweight).

You:

"Mr. Prospect, we talked about where we want to be and how we're going to feel when we get there. That's important to have that goal and to know how it makes us feel in our mind. Now let's talk about where we are currently. Your weight is the issue here. What does it feel like to be twenty pounds heavier than you should be?"

Prospect:

"I feel like crap. I feel gross."

You:

"When you say that you "feel like crap", what does feeling like crap mean to you?"

Prospect:

"I feel lazy and slow. I don't feel happy with myself."

You:

"When you look at yourself in the mirror what do you see?"

Prospect:

"An old fat dude with love handles hanging over his pants."

You:

"How does looking at those love handles hanging over your pants affect your confidence?"

Prospect:

"I feel a lot less confident."

You:

"How is feeling less confident, lazy, and unhappy with yourself affecting your life and your job?"

Prospect:

"It really makes going to work miserable and working is most of what I do."

You:

"It sounds like you have some strong motivation to really accomplish this goal. I'm excited to be able to help. Other than yourself, does anyone around you notice how overweight you are or these love handles hanging over your pants?"

Prospect:

"Yes, actually one of my good friends made a comment to me the other day that didn't feel very good."

You:

"What was it that he said?"

Prospect:

"Just that he was concerned about my weight gain."

You:

"That's great that he was concerned but yeah it's not a great feeling when other people are noticing negative things about us. What was the final straw for you? What finally made you decide to do something about your weight gain? Was it your friend's comment or something else?"

Prospect:

"Well, I've been thinking about for awhile like I said but that comment really hit home that other people are seeing me as fat. I know it's time to do something about it now."

You:

"Mr. Prospect, listen, you're doing the right thing and taking positive steps in the right direction. I'm going to encourage you to continue doing that because I've had many clients just like you become healthier and happier through our program."

This sales process can be a bit of an emotional drain for your prospect. The point of it is to get your prospect in touch with how important accomplishing this goal is. It's a workout for their mind and their emotions. It also lowers the buying resistance at the end when you are closing the sale.

The answers that your prospects are giving you are proof that they need the services that you provide. They're telling you that they need your help. If they didn't need your help, they would have already accomplished their goals without you. You are doing them a great service by being a professional who can lower the resistance and barriers to access that help.

The last thing you have to get out of the way before you give them the gym tour or trial class is their significant other. You don't want to do all this great work and then when it's time to make a buying decision they tell you that they can't without talking to their wife/Mom/Dad/significant other/etc. So let's get into the fourth and final objection.

Objection # 4: The Significant Other

The significant other objection can and will be the excuse for your prospect to not committing to the sale on the spot. We've all experienced the "I've got to talk to my wife first" just as you think you have the sale. It's one of the easiest ways of squirming out of a commitment.

But first, what about the man who arrives home to excitedly tell his wife that he's the newest member of your gym? He's happy. You're happy. His wife is not.

"You spent how much," the wife questions.

"It's only $700," the husband explains.

"Only $700? Why did you spend so much without talking to me?" She understands the power of "why."

If you remember from earlier in this book I explained to you the reasons for not quoting the price over the phone. One of those reasons is because your prospect has no sense of value for that money. They haven't experienced what you have to offer.

Now, you're forcing your newest member into that very same situation and he is far less prepared and educated on the art of selling memberships than you are! You are sending an amateur membership salesperson in to do what a professional membership salesperson should do.

One of my favorite sports is Mixed Martial Arts or what's popularly referred to as MMA. It's what is called a combat sport, like boxing. The difference between boxing and MMA, is that in MMA not only can you punch but also you can kick, throw, elbow, knee, twist your opponent's limbs, and even choke them.

I competed professionally in this sport for many years, eventually being featured on the hit TV show *The Ultimate Fighter*. In one of my fights, I knocked out a highly regarded fighter nicknamed, The Monsta. This fight lasted thirty one seconds and was featured on the syndicated TV show *Knockout Sportsworld* alongside one of my fighting idols, Mike Tyson.

After I retired from professional MMA, I dedicated myself to training others to become professional fighters. Amateurs from all walks of life would come to my gym to learn how to fight. Some would follow my advice without question. Others had to learn the hard way or what I called the "fun for me" way.

Even though these amateurs came to me to teach them, at times they had chips on their shoulders for one reason or another. Being the professional that I am, I had no problem knocking that chip straight off of their shoulder. Not only could I do it but also it was easy.

I was a professional with over twenty-five years of experience in fighting. They were amateurs who weren't even twenty-five years old most of the time. I had been fighting longer than they had been walking and breathing. Think about how easy walking and breathing is.

I don't bring this up to brag. Okay, maybe I do a little since my glory days of fighting are over but more importantly I bring this up to illustrate a point. An amateur is never as good as a professional.

When you send an amateur membership salesperson, the husband, to do what a professional membership salesperson, you, should be doing, good things very rarely happen. In my experience, you can count on one of two things happening.

If you're lucky, your new member will cancel the membership contract they just signed immediately after returning home.

In New York State, a new member has three days after they sign your contract to cancel for whatever reason that they want to. I say, "If you're lucky" because it could and sometimes will be worse.

The second of the two things that could happen is that your new member is not going to be motivated to come to your gym anymore. He's going to be reminded of the money he's "wasting" and possibly have an argument with his wife each time he comes to the gym. This will lead to him not coming, which leads to him not paying his monthly membership dues.

If you try to enforce your contract with him, he will take that anger he has about his wife's attitude and direct it towards you. He will tell his wife that he tried cancelling but this "evil" gym won't let him. He may even enlist his wife to help him badmouth you.

The next thing you know, there are bad reviews online and negative social media posts all over the Internet. This bad word of mouth costs more than cancelling his contract plus a full on television advertising campaign on top of it. All because you thought you were helping by selling him a membership.

This objection is easy to clear but a lot of salespeople forget to deal with until it's too late. Don't be that person. Sometimes it will even help you sell a membership to their significant other, as I have done many times. This objection is about making sure that your prospect can make the decision to buy a membership from you one hundred percent on their own. If they can't, it will allow you to deal with it accordingly.

Q, L, V, for the Significant Other Objection:

You:

"Ok, Mr. Prospect, you can get here, the schedule works for you, and you have significant motivation to participate in one of my programs. The last thing we need to talk about, before we do a gym tour/workout, is the people that surround you. Do you have the support of people close to you? Is there anybody in your life, a significant other or maybe a parent, that doesn't want you training or becoming a member of our gym?"

I ask whether they have supportive people around them for a few reasons. The first reason is that it's much easier to stick to your goals if people around you are supportive. It's not absolutely necessary but it definitely helps to have supportive people around you.

Another reason that I ask this is because I want them to make a decision to buy at the end of our meeting. You need them to say that either everyone around them is supportive or that they can and will make their own decision regardless of what anyone else thinks.

The final reason that I ask this is because people who are supportive may also want to become members. You're going to ask them for referrals. The first names to ask for are the ones who are supportive of your prospect going to the gym.

Prospect:

"No, everyone is supportive of me getting in shape. My buddy actually said if I do it he would too."

You:

"Ok great. We're going to hold your buddy to that and get him in here later then. So if you like our club and I can put together a program that works for you, it's your decision whether you become a member or not?"

Prospect:

"Yes."

You:

"So if you go home tonight and tell everyone around you that you became a member of our club, they are all going to be supportive of that decision?"

Prospect:

"Yes."

Write it down and proceed with your gym tour and trial workout. Obviously, the answer isn't always going to be yes. Just because they don't say yes doesn't mean that you give up. Here's an example of a time when a prospect told me about his wife not liking the idea of him training with me.

I was selling memberships to my Martial Arts school and fitness center when a guy, who we will call Rick, came in. He'd seen me on TV, watched my videos on YouTube, and was genuinely excited to be part of my studio. He hadn't even taken the trial lesson we were offering at the time.

Everything seemed to be in place. Our location as easy for him to get to and the times that we were offering classes fit in with his schedule. He had a motivating and attainable goal that he was passionate about. On top of all that, he had a great job that would have been more than likely to afford the monthly membership costs.

Then I asked him about his significant other. Rick told me that his wife had no idea he was at my gym. I asked the most powerful question in the universe ... "why?"

Rick answered, "She's not really into me training in Martial Arts."

Then I asked the second most powerful question in the universe ... "why" again.

"My wife thinks I'm going to get hurt or come home with a black eye or something," he explained. "I make the money in our household and she's afraid if something happens, I won't be able to work and I'll lose my job."

That's a pretty serious objection and can be intimidating one to overcome. My reply was to politely tell him that he wasn't going to be able to train here without his wife being okay with it.

"Sir, no offense, but I can't let you train here if your wife is that concerned about it," I replied as all of his enthusiasm left his body. "If I go ahead and sell you this membership not only am I going to get you in trouble but she might possibly get mad at me too! I do however have a solution."

The problem wasn't that his wife didn't want him getting into shape and doing something that was fun. The problem that she had was that she didn't want him getting hurt and ultimately losing his job.

I explained to Rick that getting hurt is a common misconception people have about Martial Arts training. They watch guys fight on TV and think that's what is going on for every student at the school. The reality was that less than one percent of the people that trained at my school ended up competing. And the ones that did compete, they only did so voluntarily.

"Your wife has a legitimate concern," I explained. "My solution is to invite her down here and have her watch my classes and as a matter of fact, I'll let her train right along the side of you. She will see and experience that it's actually a lot of fun and that it's not broken bones and bloody noses."

I called her on the spot from the gym. I did not let Rick make the call. As I've said before, do not let an amateur do the job of a professional.

Ring, ring, ring.

Wife:

"Hello."

Me:

"Hi ma'am, this is Erik from the Martial Arts school. I'm here with your husband and I've got to tell you that he's very excited about doing Martial Arts. He told me that you're pretty concerned about this type of training. I've explained to him that I wasn't going to let him train here if you were against it."

Wife:

"Ha-ha. Are you serious? I actually appreciate that. Yes, we have talked about this and we really can't afford him getting hurt and not being able to work."

Me:

"Yes ma'am. Rick was pretty upfront with me on this and I appreciate that. The last thing I want to do is be the source of a disagreement between you two. I know this is probably going to sound like a silly question but are you okay with him getting in better shape and working out?"

Wife:

"Yes, absolutely. I would love for him to be in better shape. I'm all for that."

Me:

"Okay, that's kind of what I thought. The reason I'm calling you is because many times people think I'm running some kind of fight club here at my Martial Arts school. The fact is ninety nine percent of the people who come to me want to lose weight and get in shape. They have jobs that they have to go to everyday. They can't be showing up with black eyes and broken bones. That is why my classes are structured to not only be effective and be fun but to be safe.

Rick is just so excited about Martial Arts that I'd like to invite you to my school to watch the training and see for yourself how safe it really is. If after you watch my classes you still feel the same way, I'll kick your husband right out of here! Ma'am would you be willing to do that, come and watch a class?"

Wife:

"Yes I would. Maybe I should try the class with him. I wouldn't mind getting in better shape and having fun too."

She ended up coming to the gym that night, participating in the class with her husband, and I sold two memberships instead of one. One that I may very well have had to cancel once Rick got home.

Rick and his wife were members of my gym for many years after that and ended up becoming pretty good friends of mine.

Once you've finished with your questions ask your prospect if they have any questions for you. Be sure to answer any questions that they may have. You are now ready to give them your gym tour and trial workout.

FREE BOOK UPDATES AND VIDEO TRAINING

This book is INTERACTIVE – to get free training videos, access to more resources, updates, and upgrades to this book when new versions or editions are released:

Text me

aosmupdates

to

(678) 506-7543

Give Them What They Want (And Need)

You cannot just tell the person that they'll get what they want by becoming a member; you must give them the experience of benefiting from it now. This is why we do gym tours and trial workouts.

Three keys to doing a great tour and trial workout:

1. Introduce your prospect to the entire staff, even the people that they may not be working with. Prospects feel more comfortable when they know the people who work at your facility and who they can go to if they need something.

2. Make sure the person who is conducting the first workout, if not you, is friendly, knowledgeable, and patient. Your new prospect may not have any experience in training so it's important that the person they are working with for the first time is good with new people.

3. Your prospect needs to get their heart rate up a little, not a lot. You want your prospect to feel good,

not like they are going to die. Getting their heart rate up boosts blood flow and gives your prospect a bit of a mood lift. That mood lift is what you're looking for because that ensures that after just one workout they are already experiencing the positive effects of training.

At the end of their workout, ask their trainer or coach how your prospect did in front of the prospect. The trainer needs to accentuate the positive. They don't need to talk about anything that your prospect struggled with during the initial workout. You don't need to hear, "this fat ass needs a lot of training so sign them up for the gold elite membership package." When your prospect hears the positive feedback from their trainer it's very encouraging and will help you in selling them a membership.

GET WHAT YOU NEED!

Everyone needs encouragement, support, and training! Join me and some of your fellow AOSM readers online at membershipsalesacademy.com. There are hours and hours of video training, interactive lessons, live lectures, and more!

You should join us by going here:

membershipsalesacademy.com

Get A Commitment

Your prospect can get to your location. The schedule that you have works for them. You got to the bottom of what they want and need. Your prospect told you that they could make a decision to buy on their own. They had a great gym tour and initial workout where their trainer gave them great feedback. You've been a passionate and professional leader throughout the process. It is now your duty to sell them a membership.

You:

"Mr. Prospect, that was great feedback from your trainer. How did you like the workout?"

Prospect:

"It was great. I loved it."

You:

"Excellent. Mr. Prospect, if I could show you a membership option that was affordable for you and fit within your budget would you want to take advantage of that now?"

Prospect:

"Yes."

You:

"Great! Grab your credit card or checking account information and we'll discuss the options that are best for you. Does that sound good?"

Or you might ask, "Ok great. Do you have your credit card info on you or is it in your car?"

Prospect:

"In my car."

You:

"Ok, go grab that and meet me in the office and we'll discuss the options that are best for you. Does that sound good?"

Prospect:

"Yes."

You:

"Ok great. I'll meet you in the office."

Presenting Membership Options

It doesn't matter how many different types of membership that your business offers. Show your prospect the best two options for them.

You just put your prospect through a mentally taxing sales process. You told them that you would help them pick a program that is best for them. If you now present all of or an exhaustive list of membership options, your prospect will feel overwhelmed at best and lied to at worst.

Sheena Iyengar, author of *The Art of Choosing*, did an experiment at a supermarket known for it's extensive product selection. She conducted this experiment at Draeger's supermarket on two consecutive Saturdays.

On the first Saturday, she set up a display that showcased twenty-four different flavors of jam. Customers had the opportunity to taste test as many as they would like to and purchase the ones that they wanted.

That Saturday, 60% of the customers that were walking by the display decided to try some jam. Of those customers that stopped, 3% actually made the decision to buy. So for every 100 customers, 60 stopped, and approximately 2 purchased jam.

The very next Saturday, Iyengar set up a display with only 6 jams available to try. The number of people that stopped at the display went down but surprising they actually had more buyers.

When 6 jams were available, 40% of Draeger's customers stopped to taste test the jams but a whopping 30% of those people decided to buy. For every 100 customers, 40 stopped, and approximately 12 bought the jam.

More choices are not always better as is the case in Iyengar's experiment. You've established yourself as an expert that understands your prospects needs. Have your prospect pick between the choices that you recommend.

Again, don't hear what I'm not saying. I'm not saying that you need to drop the amount membership options at your business. I'm saying that you need to narrow the choices down for your prospect. Give them two options. Lead them to the right buying decision and they will buy.

CHOOSE FREE BOOK UPDATES AND VIDEO TRAINING

This book is INTERACTIVE - to get free training videos, access to more resources, updates, and upgrades to this book when new versions or editions are released:

Text me

aosmupdates

to

(678) 506-7543

Getting Memberships Paid In Full

Getting paid in full (PIF) memberships is a critical piece of our business. When somebody pays in full it eliminates the cost of collecting tuition or membership dues. It provides cash flow to the business and in most cases it saves both the potential member money and the business itself money. It also eliminates any potential issues that the member may have in terms of getting behind on their membership dues.

Those are the reasons that many clubs will offer a discount to their members for PIF memberships. Additionally, they usually offer the salesperson or program director a higher commission on PIF memberships as we always did at the gyms that I worked at and eventually owned.

An important key in selling PIF memberships is remembering that what you are selling the member is worth more than what you are asking them to pay for it. If your annual memberships are in the

$1,000 range and you feel like that's expensive, you're going to struggle with selling them.

One thing that has helped me in my selling career was to reframe what I was selling in my own mind. In the book, *The Winning Mind Set* by Jim Brault and Kevin Seaman, they talk about how reframing gives you the opportunity to see difficult things from a different, more empowering perspective. They use the story of David versus Goliath.

When the Israelite soldiers looked at Goliath they thought he was so big that they couldn't kill him. When David looked at Goliath he thought that the giant was so big no attack would miss him. David went on to defeat Goliath and the idea of reframing was born!

When it comes to reframing in the art selling of memberships, I would tell myself that I'm not just selling a membership. I would look at it from the perspective of selling a solution to a serious problem in my prospect's life. Something I've said numerous times in this book already. Getting my prospect to pay $1,000 is a small amount of money for being twenty pounds lighter, for better health, for more confidence, for a better figure, etc.

As a rule you should be doing a minimum of ten percent of your business in PIF sales. It was a requirement for the salespeople in my organization. You should make it a requirement for yourself too. Personally, I would successfully close twenty percent to thirty percent of my business in PIF sales. I've had salespeople and program directors do the same thing. It works. It's proven. Use these steps and you will see your cash flow and income increase.

Step number one is to make sure that your prospect has already committed to a program. You want your new member to have already selected a number of times per week they will be coming in, the days, the times, and the monthly dues. Let's say for the sake of our example that the monthly dues for that membership are $58.

The next thing I'm going to do is show them the total amount for the whole year including the initial payment. In most states, for legal purposes, you have to show the total cost of the membership anyway.

Math:

12 months X $58 per month = $696 + $25 initiation fee = $721 total cost.

Next you're going to ask your new member to save money. How you present this question is crucial to the success of closing a PIF membership.

I do not lead with a percentage of savings or by saying, "I'll waive the initiation fee." A percentage of savings means nothing to your new member. They have to calculate that number to dollars in their head for it to mean anything to them. The last thing they want to do after going through this sales process is to do math in their head. Lead by telling the total amount of cold, hard cash you are going to save them. Money talks and everything else walks.

You:

"Mr. Member, if I could save you $122 on that membership right now would you be interested in taking advantage of saving that kind of money?"

Do you know how many people say no to the question of saving money when they have already committed to purchasing? The answer is 0.0000000001 percent. That's a number from my very own, not so scientific study. My point is that very few people are going to say no to saving money on something that they have already agreed to purchase.

Prospect:

"Yes, of course. How can I save $122?"

Now show them how those savings work. Write it down or have a PIF sell sheet already printed up so that your new member can see it with their own eyes.

You:

"Ok, Mr. Member, what I'm going to do is waive the initiation fee of $25. That brings your membership down to $696. On top of that $25 discount I'm going to take another $97 off from there. The discount is what we call a paid in full discount. Instead of 12 monthly installments you would be saving $122 by making one payment of $599. Is $599 a payment you could make today to save the $122?"

There will be many times when you will close the paid in full membership right here. If however, they say "no," reframe what making a one-time payment means and try again. I call this the "Room on Your Card Close."

You:

"You know, Mr. Member, sometimes I have members that come in and pay with their credit cards instead of using cash. If you have enough room on your credit card for a one time payment of $599, instead of making monthly payments to the club, you would just make them to your credit card company. I would still give you the $122 cash discount and your monthly payment to you credit card may even be lower than the monthly membership price. Is that an option that will work for you?"

Be quiet and let them answer. There are many times that a new member has said yes to this after initially telling me no. When you reframe it like this, the new member often realizes that they are already paying on their credit card. Instead of adding another payment (membership dues) to their monthly budget they might as well go ahead and put it on their card to save money now.

FREE BOOK UPDATES AND VIDEO TRAINING

This book is INTERACTIVE - to get free training videos, access to more resources, updates, and upgrades to this book when new versions or editions are released:

Text me

aosmupdates

to

(678) 506-7543

Closing Techniques That Get The Resistant Buyer

There are occasions when you'll get that one prospect that is going to say no to your first attempt to close the sale, no matter what. I think this type of prospect feels that they have to make you work just a little bit harder for them. You've done most of the work that you needed to do in order to get the sale. Don't give up when you meet a little bit of resistance. The finish line is right there in front of you.

It's extremely important that you get the sale today. If your prospect walks out the door without a membership, the chance of them buying it from you later goes down drastically. When I say goes down drastically, I mean the chance goes down to almost zero percent.

The next day your prospect is probably going to feel a bit sore from their initial workout. That pain in those sore muscles will outweigh the pleasure of looking better and feeling better down the road. The next thing you know they are telling themselves that being fat and overweight isn't so bad. After all, two thirds of our population is fat too. They know this because you're the one who told them that during the sales process!

Even worse, they call up their buddy and say what a great workout they had. They tell the buddy that the price is $58 per month and that they're probably going to join. The buddy, being the "helpful" buddy that he is, knows where he can get a "better deal." Even after all of that time that you spent with your prospect, they will join another club that is $5 a month cheaper. You lost them over $5 per month because you didn't close that day.

If you have determined that a membership is something that your prospect needs then you should do everything in your power to get them to "yes" right now. You're not selling a piece of junk, used car. You're not selling an overpriced vacuum cleaner. You're selling them something that is truly in their best interest to buy. You might even be saving their life. Do not feel guilty about putting some sales pressure on a prospect. It is your duty and responsibility to make sure that they become a member right now.

You Are Getting in Your Own Way Close

Earlier in the sales process when you were talking to your prospect about their goals, you asked how long they had been thinking about this goal. It could one year or one month. The amount of time really doesn't matter. Your prospect has been thinking about it and sometimes at the end of the sales process they will tell you that they "still need to think about it."

This closing technique reminds your prospect that they have been thinking about it long enough. It's time for them to commit and it's time for you to be a leader here and get them to commit.

Prospect:

"I still need to think about it."

You:

"Mr. Prospect, I understand that thinking about it is important. You told me earlier that you've been thinking about this for over a year now. You've finally taken the steps needed to stop thinking about feeling better and looking better. You're actually in the gym, doing something about it now. The schedule and location work for you. You've said that you can afford it and that you loved the workout. You've created a lot of positive momentum for yourself. Now, YOU ARE getting in YOUR OWN way. Don't do that. Keep this positive momentum going and get this membership today. Now is the best time to do it. Which payment method do you want to use to get started?"

When I Care About You More Than You Care About You Close

Sometimes when you show a prospect the price, they stop caring about the results they are going to achieve and start caring more about the expense. They are caring more about their wallet than they are about themselves. As sad as that sounds, it will happen on occasion.

Use the "When I Care About You More Than You Care About You Close" when your prospect stops caring about how important achieving their goals are.

Prospect:

"I don't know. I like your offer and everything but maybe getting in shape isn't that important to me now that I think about it."

You:

"Mr. Prospect, I appreciate the time that you've spent with me today. It's really helped me understand why you came in here for my help. Getting in shape was only part of what is important to you.

You want to be around for your grandkids for a long time to come. I care about helping you do that. You want to be able to go upstairs without feeling like you're having a heart attack. I care about helping you do that.

It actually seems to me that *I* care more about *YOU* getting in shape than *YOU* do. When I care about you more than you care about you, you need to let me help. Get your membership right now and let's continue the progress and positive momentum that we have made towards those goals already. Which payment option would you like to use to get started today?"

My Life Isn't Going To Change Close

The "My Life Isn't Going To Change Close" works great for that prospect that likes to put you on the defense. The prospect will downplay how much you care or just doesn't believe that you care at all. They also love confrontation. They use confrontation as a way to throw you off of your game and to test your genuineness. Use this closing technique to let your prospect be right and close the sale anyway.

Prospect:

"You just want me to become a member to make a commission."

You:

"Yes, Mr. Prospect, you are correct. I'm going to make a commission when you become a member today. This is my job and I'm paid well to do it. The thing is that you becoming a member today will not change my lifestyle one bit. You becoming a member today will not buy me a new car. You becoming a member today will not get me a bigger house. You becoming a member today will not change my life except for the fact that I know that I will be helping *you* to change *yours*. You will be looking better and feeling better. That is why I do this and why I'm so passionate about it. Which payment option do you want to use today to become a member?"

Show Me the Money Close

Occasionally you will run into a prospect that makes enough money to afford your membership but their monthly budget is tapped for other things. I've successfully used the Show Me the Money Close to not only get the sale but to also save them money in their monthly budget. I call it the Show Me the Money Close because it involves your prospect showing you where they spend their money so that you can help them direct some wasteful spending towards their new membership.

Prospect:

"I really like what you have to offer. I just simply doesn't fit into my budget right now."

You:

"Mr. Prospect, I'm glad that you like my offer. You like it because it's a fair offer and you know that we can help you accomplish your goal of losing twenty pounds. Is that correct?"

Prospect:

"Yes, but I don't really have that much in my budget right now."

You:

"When you decided to come here you had to have had a certain expectation of what you were able to afford. How much was it that you were planning on for your monthly membership payment?"

Prospect:

"Well I was thinking it would be around $40 per month. I know I can handle that but $65 per month is just a bit out of my budget."

You:

"I understand. If I came into a place expecting to pay $40 and found out that it was $65 it would make me pause for a minute too. So the difference between you becoming a member or not is $25?"

Prospect:

"Yes, that's about it. $25 a month is quite a bit outside of my budget."

You:

"Ok, yes. I understand. It sounds like you understand the value of staying within your budget. Mr. Prospect, would you agree that I've been very honest and helpful in my dealing with you today?"

Prospect:

"Yes you have. Why do you ask?"

You:

"And you have been honest and helpful with me today as well. The reason that I ask is because I'm going to ask you to continue on being honest and helpful with me today as we see if we can figure out how to make this membership work for the $6 a week that we are talking about here. Will you do that for me right now?"

Prospect:

"Sure, why not."

You:

"Well, Mr. Prospect, I want you to give me a list of three things that you buy every month. The first thing is something that you probably can't do without. The second thing is something you love but could definitely do without. The last thing would be something you definitely do not need to buy this month. Let me give you an example. For me, something that I probably couldn't do without each month would be cable TV. I'd probably go crazy if I didn't get my fix of *The Real Housewives of Beverly Hills*. I spend about $150 per month on cable. What is something that you probably can't do without?"

Prospect:

"I would say my car payment. I really need to get back and forth to where I'm going."

You:

"Ok, yes, that's understandable. What would you say is something that you love to buy each much but could definitely do without?"

Prospect:

"That's a little bit harder but I would say Starbucks coffee. I don't really need to go to Starbucks every morning but I love their coffee."

You:

"And what you say is the thing that you could do without and it wouldn't really matter that much?"

Prospect:

"I would say going out to lunch everyday. I could probably bring my lunch to work."

You:

"Very good. You might have just solved your $6 a week dilemma yourself. The average lunch costs between $8-$15 per day. What do you think about this? What if instead of never going out to lunch let's take baby steps. Let's cut it back and use it as a reward for yourself. Instead of going out everyday, you go out to lunch at the end of the week. If, and only if, you make all of your training sessions. This will amount to saving between $30-$60 per week. That amount not only covers the $6 per week we were trying to cover but also pays for your entire membership. In fact it pays for our Elite membership. Let's get this membership in place for you today so you can start looking better, feeling better, and saving money! Do you want to use your credit card or checking account for this?"

Not My Favorite Close

One of the program director jobs that I worked was at this fitness center in Syracuse, NY. It was a little gym that didn't have much to offer in the way of equipment and amenities. Three or four of our competitors had huge open spaces with tons of equipment and beautiful swimming pools. Guess what I heard about? Yup, that we don't have a swimming pool. Oh man, how these prospects really needed a swimming pool. I would also hear that we didn't have a certain favorite type of cardio equipment now and then. At other times it would be that I want to take, insert a favorite program that we don't offer, cardio kickboxing, yoga, etc.

There are just some prospects that you are going to deal with that love pointing out all of the things that you do not offer. It's not that they don't want to train at your club, many times it's that they are setting you up to get a deal or to put off making a decision. Guess what? I still sold memberships. Here's how I did it and how you can too.

You:

"Mr. Prospect, we all have our favorites in life and I understand that not seeing a swimming pool / piece of equipment here may be a bit disappointing. What is it that you think you will get out of using a swimming pool / equipment?"

Prospect:

"Well, I heard / know that swimming pools / equipment are great for improving cardio."

You:

"You are right. They / It is great for improving cardio. Is there anything else about a swimming pool / equipment that are important to you?"

Prospect:

"No, it's just that good cardio training is important losing weight so I would like to join a club that has a swimming pool / equipment."

You:

"Yes, cardiovascular exercise is going to help you accomplish your goal. That is the reason I feel we have the perfect membership for you. We've had many people come here and have a similar thought. Someday we may even install a swimming pool / equipment. Although we may not have a swimming pool / equipment right now, we do have something that is a lot better for accomplishing your goals. Ultimately, that is what you came here for is to accomplish your goals. What will help you with that even more than a swimming pool / equipment is ... (explain your alternative to swimming pool / equipment). Besides having an alternative that has proven results for other members like you, our gym is clean, and our staff is friendly. Your success is not dependent on a swimming pool / equipment but the things I've just mentioned. Wouldn't you agree?"

Prospect:

"Yes, I guess you do have a point."

You:

"Let's finish up getting your membership squared away and I'll help you become more familiar with (alternative equipment / program). I'm sure once you see the results you get from it, it will be your new favorite piece of equipment / program. Does that sound good to you?"

Prospect:

"Yes it does."

You:

"Ok, great. Are you using your credit card to get this membership or your checking account?"

You're Pressuring Me Close

<u>**Prospect:**</u>

"I feel like you're just pressuring me to get the sale. I don't want to make a decision under pressure and then regret it later."

<u>**You:**</u>

"Let me apologize. I believe in what I do because I have helped hundreds of people with the same problems and challenges that you have, accomplish their goals. This belief and passion for what I do is coming across as me putting pressure on you. That is not what I want you to feel. The other thing I don't want you to feel is regret.

I know that we can help you lose this twenty pounds. You know that we can help too. If I let you walk out the door without helping you I would feel terrible but more than that, you will regret not continuing with the positive momentum that you've started today.

Ma'am sometimes we mistake motivation and passion for pressure. You see, motivation and passion is exactly what you need to accomplish your goals so do not be afraid of it.

Let's get this membership now and continue to work towards accomplishing your goals. Being motivated and being passionate is the only way to do it. Do you understand what I'm saying here?"

Prospect:

"Yes I do."

You:

"Ok, great. Do you want to use your checking account or your credit card to set this up today?"

That's The Reason Close

If you've followed the sales process correctly it's very rare that you get a prospect that brings up their fear of commitment. Sometimes however, you still may get this one at the end.

This closing technique takes something negative that the prospect says about themselves or about the situation and makes it a reason for becoming a member.

Prospect:

"I'm just afraid that I'm going to quit. I always start something and then end up not finishing or quitting."

You:

"Ma'am, we've all been quitters at something in our lives. The reason we quit is two fold. One, we are not getting the results that we wanted and two, nobody is supporting our journey to help us keep going. Would you agree with me on that?"

Prospect:

"Yes I would."

You:

"Ma'am, you have an amazing goal, a goal that is going to require you to put in a bit of work. Work that is going to be supported by me and my awesome staff here at Name Fitness.

If you find yourself quitting all the time then that is the reason that I'm telling you to become a member today. We are going to make sure that you lose those twenty pounds and when it seems like you need to quit, we will be here to support and encourage you to continue.

Ma'am, I have many former quitters in my gym right now. They are also former fat people. Now give yourself some credit here. If you really were a quitter, you wouldn't even have came to my gym today. Right?"

Prospect:

"I guess you're right."

You:

"Now tell me which payment option you'd like to use to finish setting up your membership today."

Answer For Everything Close (aka, The Zig Ziglar)

I often refer to this close as the Zig Ziglar because I learned it from his book, *Secrets of Closing the Sale*. It's a great book and if you haven't read it, you need to.

This close is for when you get that prospect that uses a compliment to get you off track. Don't let the Mr. Nice Guy persona derail your selling of a membership. Thank them for the compliment and use the "Zig Ziglar Close" to get the sale.

<u>Prospect:</u>

"You're a great salesperson. No matter what I say, you have an answer for it but I'm just not sure that I'm ready to buy."

<u>You:</u>

"Mr. Prospect, I appreciate that compliment but there are many things that I do not have an answer for. That's one of the reasons why I'm so excited to offer you this opportunity to become a member today.

This membership *is* the answer to *your* problem. If you didn't like the training, couldn't get here, and didn't have a real goal I wouldn't even offer you a membership but the facts are that you do.

Take advantage of this opportunity and become a member right now. Will you do that with your credit card or with your checking account?"

FREE BOOK UPDATES AND VIDEO TRAINING

This book is INTERACTIVE - to get free training videos, access to more resources, updates, and upgrades to this book when new versions or editions are released:

Text me

aosmupdates

to

(678) 506-7543

Referrals: The Silver Bullets of Selling

The Lone Ranger was a TV Western that was a phenomenon in the 1950's. He wasn't your normal kind of gun slinging, super hero though. He always used proper English, he never drank alcohol, and he never smoked. He represented purity. Even when The Lone Ranger used his gun against an opponent he didn't even shoot to kill. Instead, he used silver bullets to disarm his opponents as quickly as possible.

In selling, referrals from new or current members are the silver bullets of your sales process. Due to the fact that the referral knows the person who referred them, referrals are the quickest and easiest way to disarm a prospect's resistance to your pitch. Many times the person who gave you the referral pre-qualifies them. They are probably in a similar income bracket and probably have similar needs. Referrals are also free. They don't require any investment other than your time.

Referrals in the fitness industry have to be handled very carefully. If you are doing your job in a professional way, you will be able to ask for referrals in many different situations. Do a great job and ask the right way and your members will be happy to give you referrals on a regular basis. The keys are to know when to ask, know how to ask, and know what to say when you contact the referral.

Knowing when to ask is simple, ask all of the time. Salespeople at my gyms were required to ask for referrals at least four different times within thirty days of their first contact with a prospect. There are some who disagree and say that is too much. They say you should keep your asking to a minimum and only when your customer has had proven results.

The first thirty days is when your new member is the most excited and enthusiastic about your club. Waiting for your new member to get the results they are looking for might take a while. Plus, there are a lot of factors to their success that are beyond your control. What if you're new member has to stop training for medical reasons? You waited and now your opportunity to ask is gone.

Asking for the referral in the proper way is the key to getting the referral. You are, in essence, asking someone to hand over information about one of their friends. Sensitive information at that, so trust is extremely important. The person giving you the referral needs to trust that you're going to handle their friend with care and sensitivity. They are going to judge you on this by how you handled them when they became a member.

Once you've been able to get a referral from a member have one shot to make a good impression. It's similar to a fact-to-face opportunity in that respect. What you say and how you say it here is just as important, if not more than any of the other steps in handling a referral. Nobody wants a call from a salesperson that says, "Hey, your friend Jamie said you need to lose some weight off of that fat ass of yours. Is that true?" So let's get specific with the when, how, and what to say of dealing with referrals.

Eight Ways To Get Referrals and How To Turn Them Into Appointments

There are four basic parts to getting referrals and turning them into appointments. They are:

1. Asking for the referral.

2. Contacting the referral.

3. Permission to continue.

4. Closing the appointment.

If you get a referral within the first three attempts, wait until thirty days after they have been training with you to ask for another referral.

1) When your prospect books their first appointment with you.

You might be saying to yourself, "but you said that trust is important to getting a referral. How is there any trust if you haven't even got to the first appointment yet?"

You were able to get your prospect to commit to an appointment with you. That's enough trust. Ask them for the referral.

You:

"Mrs. Prospect, sometimes people really enjoy working out with someone that's already a friend of theirs. Do you have a friend that might have a similar goal that would be interested in coming in to workout alongside you?"

If the prospect responds with a "no," it's important to remind them that it's not a requirement to have a workout partner. If they get the impression that it takes two people and they can't think of anyone, your prospect might not show up.

Prospect:

"No, not really."

You:

"Ok, it's not a big deal, you don't need a workout partner to do this. I just wanted to ask just in case you knew someone. We'll see you later today at 4 pm."

If they respond with a "yes," then get their friends contact information so you can handle it personally. Remember, you are the professional salesperson, not your prospect. You want to be the one to contact the referral.

Prospect:

"Yes, I do actually. I think my friend Sally would be interested in coming."

You:

"Awesome, that'd be great. I will give her a buzz as soon as I'm off the phone with you. I'm going to keep it simple when I call her. I'm going to let her know that you are coming in today at 4 pm and see if she wants to come in and workout with you. What number can Sally be reached?"

Prospect:

"That's great. Her number is ..."

You:

"Thank you, Mrs. Prospect. I'll call you back and let you know if you can expect Sally to come in with you today at 4. If not, I'll see you either way. Thanks again. I'm looking forward to meeting you in person."

Calling the prospect's referral:

You:

"Hi Sally, your friend, Mrs. Prospect is coming in to Name Fitness today to get a workout it. Mrs. Prospect thought that you might have fun working out with her and asked me to invite you. My name is Erik and I'll be working with you two today. Would you be interested in getting a workout in with Mrs. Prospect today?"

If the referral says "yes," then you handle it the exact same way that I outlined earlier in this book under Telephone Mastery. If the referral says "no," try to get a time for them to come in that is more convenient.

Sally:

"She did huh? Haha. Well I really can't today, I'm very busy."

You:

"Ah ok, I understand. It is kind of last minute. Do you mind if I ask if trying a workout at a time that is more convenient for you is something you would be interested in?"

Sally:

"Yes, I have been thinking about joining a gym. What other times are available?"

You:

"I have open tomorrow at noon or 5:30 pm. Which time is best for you?"

Sally:

"I'll take tomorrow at noon."

You:

"Ok great. Tomorrow at noon it is. So let me ask you Sally, is working out going to be a new thing for you or have to trained before?"

From here you continue with your Telephone Mastery skills. When you call back Mrs. Prospect, let her know that her friend Sally will be coming on a different day but Mrs. Prospect is more than welcome to do that workout for free as well. It's your way of saying thank you for the referral.

2) When your prospect comes in for their appointment.

When people have an appointment booked with you, unless they're a hermit, they will tell other people. The people that they tell about the appointment are potential referrals. Ask them for the referral before you get into the sales process as part of your small talk.

You:

"Hi Mrs. Prospect, welcome to Name Fitness. Are you excited to get started?"

Prospect:

"Yes, I am!"

You:

"What do your friends and family think about you coming here today and about your new goals? Are they excited for you?"

Prospect:

"Yes, they are. They've been very supportive."

You:

"When we talked on the phone previously I asked if you had a friend that might want to come in with you. At the time, you didn't have anyone you could think of. What about one of your family or friends that's excited for you? I would invite them in and offer them a free workout courtesy of you. Who do you think would take advantage of it?"

Prospect:

"Now that you mention it, yes. My friend Sally would probably do it."

You:

"Ok, great. I will give her a call while you're doing your workout today. I'll let her know that because she seemed so excited about you working out that you wanted to give her a free workout as well. What number can Sally be reached?"

Prospect:

"Ok sounds good. Her number is ..."

Calling the prospect's referral:

<u>**You:**</u>

"Hi Sally, this is Erik from Name Fitness. You're friend, Mrs. Prospect, is here working out right now. She told me that you were really supportive of her getting in better shape and losing weight. As a thank you for being such a supportive friend, Mrs. Prospect wanted me to reach out to you and offer you a free (offer) as well. Would getting a free (offer) today or tomorrow be something that interests you?"

3) When your prospect becomes a member.

You ask for this referral after you have completed the entire sales process and received your new member's payment. Let me warn you though, do not let asking for the referral get in the way of closing the prospect that you have in front of you right now. Make sure you finish closing the new member first.

You:

"Welcome to Name Fitness, Mrs. Prospect! I've asked you a couple times if you had any friends that might want to come here and workout with you. I ask because working out with friends can be a lot of fun but also because word of mouth if very important to my success here. Now that you've become a member and had the chance to see how I conduct business you can see that I'm professional, courtesy, and very humble. Haha. I will treat any person you refer to me in the same professional and courteous way. I'm still willing to offer a friend of yours a free (offer). What friend would you like me to offer this to?"

4) 30 days after your new member has started training.

At this point in your new member's training, they should see and feel some positive results. Their friends may start noticing that your new member has lost some weight. Maybe your new member is feeling the effects of an elevated mood and self-esteem. Ask them and then ask them for a referral.

You:

"Mrs. Prospect, you're looking good. How are you feeling about your program?"

New Member:

"I'm feeling great about it. I've already lost ten pounds!"

You:

"That's great! I'm proud of you and happy that I was able to help you make progress on your fitness goals. Have any of your friends noticed and would any of them be interested in losing ten pounds in their first thirty days of training with us?"

5) 90 days after your new member has started training.

When you get to the ninety-day mark with your new member, you ask for a referral in a similar fashion that you did at the thirty-day mark. Ask them about their results and see if there is a friend that would like to realize similar results.

Asking the same way here as you did at the thirty-day mark is important because new friends may have came into the picture now. Your new member is looking better and feeling better. They may even be hanging out with new people. Those new people are a great source of referrals. Sometimes old friends will wait to see if your new member is going to stick it out as well. Now that ninety days have passed, your new member may have some friends who see that they won't be left alone if they become a member too.

6) When a member has shared a success story with you.

If you are following this sales process, you will be very successful salesperson in the art of selling memberships. This will mean that you will have members who will be successful as well. They will lose weight, get in shape, feel better about the way they look, have increased confidence and more.

There is a saying that goes, "success breeds success." Tell people about your successes with others and people will want to be part of that success as well. When a member achieves a goal or shares a success story with you, it's the perfect time to ask for a referral.

Your member will be happy that they have achieved the goal they set out to accomplish. They will also feel a lot better about referring someone else to you because your plan actually worked for them. Ask them to help you help others become as successful as they are.

You:

"Congratulations, Mrs. Member! I love hearing about the successes of my clients and I'm so proud of you. Are you as proud of yourself as I am?"

Mrs. Member:

"Yes, I am."

You:

"Do any of your friends and family know about your success?"

Mrs. Member:

"Yes, a few of them do."

You:

"Are they proud of you?"

Mrs. Member:

"Yes, they are. It's a great feeling."

You:

"That is great. Mrs. Member, you've known me for a little bit now. You've experienced excellent results with our program. You know what I say; I do, because you've had the opportunity to experience it first hand. Let me ask you, who is it amongst your family or friends that you think I could really help out?"

7) When a member has shared a challenge that they are having.

Let's be honest, not everyone is going to have an easy path to successfully accomplishing his or her goals. There are bumps in the path along the way. These bumps or challenges that your new member will face are great opportunities for and for them. Helping your member through these challenges will endear them to your program and will lead to you getting referrals.

Mr. Member:

"I'm having trouble staying motivated / getting through my workouts / getting to the gym / etc, etc."

You:

"Mr. Member, why is it that you are having these challenges?"

Let them talk. Many times they will talk and realize that they are challenges that only exist in their minds. Let your member get if off their chest and just listen. Whatever their answer is your reply will be similar each time.

You:

"Mr. Member, we all face these challenges when we do something that is worthwhile. There isn't a single person in this gym that has not had to overcome some sort of setback or challenge. You've had to do it from day one here. Let's not forget that. You had to overcome some obstacles just to become a member!

One thing that could really help you overcome these challenges is finding a workout partner. Working out with someone else helps your workouts to be more motivating and also gives coming to the gym a new sense of purpose. When you're your friend's workout partner, you are motivated to help them and in the process you are helping yourself as well.

Mr. Member, I'd be more than happy to give one of your friends or family members a free week of training to help you. How awesome would it be to help yourself while helping out a friend as well? Who do you know that would like to get in shape or lose weight?"

8) When your member has to cancel their membership.

It happens, members have to cancel memberships from time to time. Before I let anyone cancel, I always set up a meeting beforehand. I want to know if canceling is something we can work through or if it really has to happen.

Every club has a cancellation policy and more times than not a cancellation fee that goes along with it. I've always used this policy at the places I've worked to help me get referrals.

<u>**You:**</u>

"Mr. Member, I'm sorry to hear that you have to cancel your membership. As I explained to you when you signed up for your membership, there is a cancellation fee. That fee is $89 / 60 days notice / etc. Now before I go ahead and initiate this, I have an opportunity to make a trade with you so that you don't have to pay the cancellation fee at all. Would you be interested in that?"

Mr. Member:

"Yes, of course. If there is something I can do so that I don't have to pay the fee, I'd be happy to do it."

You:

"Ok, great. What I can do is go to my manager / billing company / etc. I'll explain your situation and that you just cannot fulfill your agreement at this time. I will also bring them five names of people who would want to "take over" your membership. So to my manager / billing company / etc., it's not even really like a cancellation but more like a transfer of a membership. I'm going to need your help with those five names. Who do you know that may be interested in losing weight or getting in shape and could use a membership to your gym?"

From here, you can work the deal however you would like. If they give you five names, you waive the cancellation fee. You could make it contingent upon at least two of them coming in for a trial workout or one of them signing up. You don't technically have the referral take over the old member's agreement. You cancel the old member and sign up the referral as a new member. This technique has worked successfully for me and is one of the reasons why I ask members to meet with me before they cancel.

FREE BOOK UPDATES AND VIDEO TRAINING

This book is INTERACTIVE - to get free training videos, access to more resources, updates, and upgrades to this book when new versions or editions are released:

Text me

aosmupdates

to

(678) 506-7543

Do, Be, Do, Be, Do

I think Frank Sinatra said it best when he sang the words, "do, be, do, be, do." If you want to be a master, you have to do what the masters do. Do, be, do, be, do.

To truly master any skill you must learn, practice, fail, and learn again, practice again. In the process of doing, you become a master.

What I've taught you in this book must be applied. Have patience with yourself when you are applying the strategies and skills that I've laid out. Know and understand that all masters must first be terrible at whatever it is that they are attempting to master.

The good part about what you've learned from this book is that it's not some fairy tale that I've dreamt up. The knowledge comes from experience and applying the skills and techniques within. The art of selling memberships has been proven over and over to close sales and make money for those that apply themselves and keep practicing if at first you don't get it exactly right.

Take the knowledge from this book and practice it. Practice on your spouse or significant other. Practice in the mirror but ultimately, practice in the real world in front of a prospect. That's the time when the practice becomes doing and doing becomes being.

Coming from an industry where we all understand the value of a coach, you may want a coach to help you or your organization with closing sales. Who better to have coach you than the man that wrote the book on it? I'm available for talks via seminars, workshops, and webinars. I will work one on one or with a group, large or small. If you want to supercharge your sales closing contact me via email at erik@sellingmemberships.com. It would be my pleasure to work with you. In the meantime, do, be, do, be, do!

FREE BOOK UPDATES AND VIDEO TRAINING

This book is INTERACTIVE – to get free training videos, access to more resources, updates, and upgrades to this book when new versions or editions are released:

Text me

aosmupdates

to

(678) 506-7543

Made in the USA
Las Vegas, NV
03 February 2023

66823186R00125